By the same author

You Are What You Eat
You Are What You Eat Cookbook
Dr Gillian McKeith's Ultimate Health Plan
Dr Gillian McKeith's Shopping Guide

Gillian
McKeith's

Wedding
Countdown
Diet

How to look and feel
amazing on your big day

MICHAEL JOSEPH
an imprint of PENGUIN BOOKS

MICHAEL JOSEPH

Published by the Penguin Group
Penguin Books Ltd, 80 Strand, London WC2R 0RL, England
Penguin Group (USA) Inc., 375 Hudson Street, New York, New York 10014, USA
Penguin Group (Canada), 90 Eglinton Avenue East, Suite 700, Toronto, Ontario, Canada M4P 2Y3
(a division of Pearson Penguin Canada Inc.)
Penguin Ireland, 25 St Stephen's Green, Dublin 2, Ireland (a division of Penguin Books Ltd)
Penguin Group (Australia), 250 Camberwell Road,
Camberwell, Victoria 3124, Australia (a division of Pearson Australia Group Pty Ltd)
Penguin Books India Pvt Ltd, 11 Community Centre,
Panchsheel Park, New Delhi – 110 017, India
Penguin Group (NZ), 67 Apollo Drive, Rosedale, North Shore 0632, New Zealand
(a division of Pearson New Zealand Ltd)
Penguin Books (South Africa) (Pty) Ltd, 24 Sturdee Avenue,
Rosebank, Johannesburg 2196, South Africa

Penguin Books Ltd, Registered Offices: 80 Strand, London WC2R 0RL, England

www.penguin.com

First published 2007
1

Copyright © Gillian McKeith, 2007

The moral right of the author has been asserted

Designed by Smith & Gilmour, London
Photography by Dan Jones
Illustrations by Izumi Nogawa@dutchuncle
Printed in Great Britain by Butler and Tanner Ltd, Frome, Somerset

A CIP catalogue record for this book is available from the British Library

ISBN: 978-0-718-15313-7

Every effort has been made to ensure the information in this book is accurate.
The views and advice in this book are based on the author's training in complementary
therapy. The information in this book will be relevant to the majority of people but
may not be applicable in each individual case, so it is advised that professional medical
help is obtained for specific information on personal health matters. Neither the
publisher nor the author accept any legal responsibility for any personal injury
or other damage or loss arising from the use or misuse of the information and
advice in this book. All vitamin, mineral and herbal supplements are sold in
varying strengths, so always check the dosage on the packaging.

CONTENTS

PART 1 I DO

INTRODUCTION

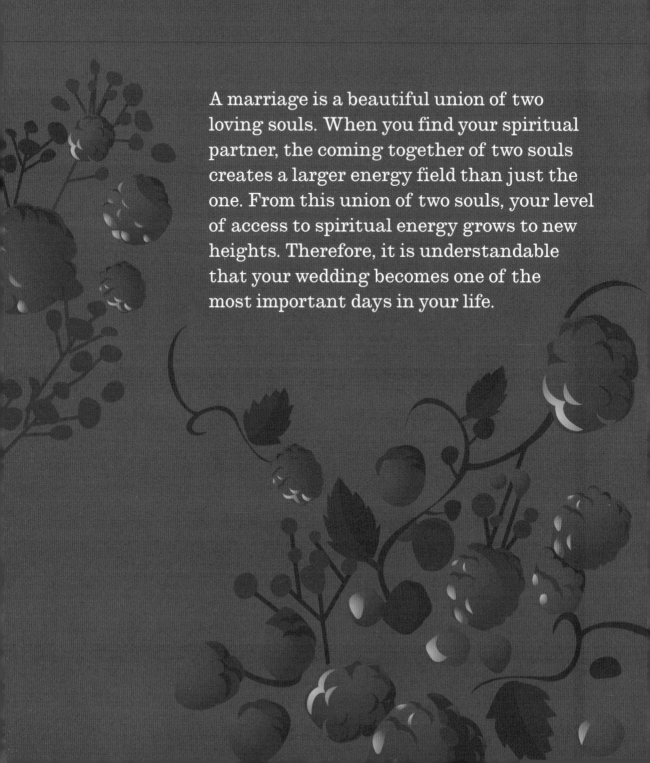

A marriage is a beautiful union of two loving souls. When you find your spiritual partner, the coming together of two souls creates a larger energy field than just the one. From this union of two souls, your level of access to spiritual energy grows to new heights. Therefore, it is understandable that your wedding becomes one of the most important days in your life.

This is truly a special milestone in your life. I know that you want to feel your best and look fabulous on your big day. It all means so much. In the days leading up to your wedding, you will need the energy and inner strength to cope with whatever is thrown at you along the way. The healthier you eat and the more that you take care of yourself overall, the better equipped you will be to handle the immense preparations as well as the enormous emotional, psychological, mental and physical toll of the Big Day. Take it from me, someone who has helped many brides: weddings can be magnets for trouble.

The unexpected has a funny way of showing up at the wrong time, like right before your special day. You can either cope well or fly into a total tizz. If you live with poor food choices and a bad diet, it will be impossible for you to be relaxed, focused or in control of the situation or yourself. Please don't reach for the comfort foods, booze and the chocolate bars to 'get through'. You will end up spotty, grumpy and bursting at the seams. Any crisis, small or large, that rears its ugly head just before the wedding will send you into orbit if you are not eating well. The nutritionally deficient are unable to handle stress and lack vital energy. Poor eaters cannot think clearly, as their brains lack vital nourishment, and I'm afraid junk food addicts tend to wobble rather than glide down the aisle. When you embrace my good food lifestyle, you will look great, feel wonderful and deal with anything at all.

I will let you in on a story of my own. I anointed myself as the wedding maven for my own event. I wanted mine to be the ace of all shows, the smash hit of Broadway, the Hollywood Oscar winner, the Mother of all Weddings! I laboured for months to find the best caterer, wedding dress, violinist, Scottish bagpipe player kitted out with kilt, Manhattan dancers complete with four acrobatic players, two diva opera singers to perform *Phantom*, solo cellist along with renowned mini orchestra and a number one rock band. It was Operation Wedding, Gillian-style. I had become 'Bridezilla'.

The flowers were no different. I had searched for weeks to find the most creative and eclectic flower designer in all the land. I interviewed one florist arranger after another until I finally found 'the one'.

The morning of my Big Event arrives. It's the Wedding Day. I am at 'Command Central', the ceremonial hall, at sunrise to instruct my buzzing team. Everything was going according to plan, like clockwork. The ten bridesmaids were all in a row perched on high chairs as make-up artists furiously painted their faces. Hair stylists were intensely coiffing. The tailor was pressing and steaming gowns. The food was being chopped, diced, sautéed, tossed and meticulously placed on silver platters. I was in the middle of the fray – and that's when I got the call.

FLORIST: 'Hi Gillian. I can't do your wedding.'
GILLIAN: [In horror, I screech] 'What do you mean?!'
FLORIST: 'I under-priced your wedding. I just can't do it.'
   [In resigning but emphatic tone]
GILLIAN: 'I don't understand. I already paid you everything in advance.'
FLORIST: 'Well, honey. I can't come unless you pay me three times the amount.
GILLIAN: 'I spent every last dime. I have nothing left.'
FLORIST: 'I am cancelling. I can't be there. Goodbye, sweetheart. And good luck.'

The gravity of the flowerless day started to sink in. This would mean no specially designed bouquets for the bride, no posies for the ten bridesmaids, no hand-helds for the four flower girls, no horseshoe for the page-boy, nothing adorning the aisle, stripped ushers, no table arrangements, not even a buttonhole flower for my groom, no petals would be anywhere in sight. What a stark thought. Just hours before my walk down the aisle, it was clearly too late to get another florist. A bride without flowers is worse than a bride with no groom, I pondered.

Thank heavens, however, I had spent three months prior to my wedding day on a superfood healthy eating regime. I had specially designed my food plan to strengthen me for the most momentous day of my life. Mentally, physically, emotionally, I felt like I could conquer anything. When your body is in the right shape from the right foods, then everything else comes into line. So on this very morning instead of collapsing in a ball of tears from the stress of the situation, I stopped, collected myself and went into commando mode. If I had not taken care of myself, I would have been a withering mess. I mustered up all my strength.

A lightbulb switched on in my head. I realized that there was another bride in the hall next door just finishing her walk down her own aisle. She was the scheduled early wedding, while mine was the late afternoon one. I burst out from the doors running just as she was getting into the wedding carriage with her new beau. I explained that my wedding was to take place in the afternoon but the florist had just cancelled on me that morning. 'Can I buy your flowers from you as your ceremony is now over?' I pleaded. The new bride presented an even better solution as she offered, 'I can't take your money. Please use my flowers and have a wonderful wedding day.' The carriage quickly departed. She left every last flower for my wedding!

The moral of my story is that all weddings attract craziness. So it's vital to be ready and prepared. There is no better way to prepare yourself on all levels than to start with your diet and your lifestyle. What you eat is the foundation of everything. In this book, I give all brides, even grooms, and your family and friends too, every piece of help to get ready for the Big Day. A slim, toned body, radiant skin and glossy, vital hair, a happy attitude, calm emotions and strength of spirit, it is all within your reach even if the Day seems bigger than you. Follow my Wedding Countdown Diet and you will truly be the Belle of the Ball and the Queen of your Castle. You will feel it, you will look it and you will be it.

Wishing you Love and Light on your Special Day and Every Day,

Gillian

GILLIAN McKEITH, PhD   www.drgillianmckeith.com

GOAL-SETTING

Rarely have I met a bride-to-be who doesn't want to lose some weight – a little or a lot – and tone up before she ties the knot. But it's not just size that matters. You want to look and feel your very best in every way. When I ask my clients to give me their wedding wish lists, the responses go something like this: 'I have to be a size 10 with a tiny waist and a flat stomach. I need perfect skin, glossy hair, a dazzling smile. I want to look pretty and feel awake all day and have the time of my life . . .' You get the idea. **Do I laugh at their lengthy requests? On the contrary. I tell them, as I tell you, that anything is possible.** My most recent TV bride, Lisa, told me that her biggest fear was that she would have to walk down the aisle sideways as she might get jammed between the pews. This fear had caused her to reschedule her wedding day twice! When I met her she had no wedding date in sight.

But as anyone who's familiar with my food philosophy knows, when you truly embrace my healthy way of living, the results are far-reaching. I won't wave my magic wand and make your dreams a reality. But *you can*, if you follow my advice.

What Sort of Bride Do You Want to Be?

Before you embark on my Wedding Countdown, I need you to set some goals. You stand more chance of realizing your dreams if you know what they are in the first place. So your first step is to think about what you really want for yourself for your big day. Not just 'I want to be thin'; let's get specific.

Don't be negative. Think of your best points, and how they can be enhanced.

Maybe you love your curves – your sexy cleavage and sensual hips – but your under-eye bags and tired grey skin are letting you down. Perhaps you're always getting compliments on your great complexion, but losing that spare couple of inches round your waist and hips would make your day. Or maybe, as I find with many people I see, you've got the makings of a beautiful bride, but you've become lazy about your health and you're suffering from spots, bloating and cellulite.

It can be hard to be objective about your appearance, especially if your self-esteem is low, as I find it often is in clients who aren't looking after themselves. So ask your friends, family and husband-to-be for their input. What do they think your plus points are? You're not asking them for criticism, just a nod in the right direction. If a straw poll proves people love your long, curly locks, for example, then for heaven's sake don't have them cut off!

Look into Your Crystal Ball

I'm a real believer in visualization. It's one of the best ways to focus your mind on what you want – *and* one of the best ways of achieving it. It works for my weight-conscious clients and can work for you too. Visualization is a powerful tool used by successful business people, politicians, athletes and performers the world over. Put simply, what you see is what you get. In effect, we are all in control of our destiny. It then starts with a dream, then a vision and then a manifestation.

First, you can use it to look into your future and see your wedding day as you'd like it to be. This will help you set your Countdown Goals. Then, you can use visualization to make those goals happen. Five minutes is all you need.

Start with some relaxation – a relaxed state of mind is the best way to turn off the outside world and tune in to your inner self.

Take the phone off the hook and make sure no one will disturb you. Sit comfortably or lie down in a quiet place. Close your eyes. Inhale deeply through your nose for a count of five. Hold for five. For a further count of five exhale through your mouth. Follow the breath. Listen to your breath. Repeat this sequence ten times to slow your breathing and quiet your mind. Focus only on the breath.

Now visualize your wedding day. See yourself getting ready in the morning: having your make-up and hair done, stepping into your bridal gown, positioning your veil. Take a long look at yourself in front of a full-length mirror. See yourself radiant and smiling, witness how your clothes enhance your figure.

Then perhaps you're in the car going to the church or register office . . . you're entering the building . . . you're at the top of the aisle. Use all your senses as you imagine the day unfolding. How does the luxurious fabric of your gown feel against your skin? How do the flowers smell? Hear the sighs and murmurs as guests catch sight of you. Picture your fiancé's expression as you near his side; taste the champagne as you sip your first glass as husband and wife. Note how wonderful you feel.

Make this visualization as bold and colourful and real as it can possibly be. Be there in the moment, experience it. And remember: this is *your* dream so nothing can go wrong; everything will happen as you want it to.

Slowly open your eyes.

Set Your Goals

So what did you see? What were the major differences between the image you just saw, and how you are today? How did you feel, healthwise, in comparison?

Take a pen and paper and write down everything you can think of, and don't forget your emotions. You may have just a few 'wants' or you may go into double figures. But chances are they will fall in to distinct categories, such as body, mind, health and beauty.

Try to narrow these down into five 'must-haves'. These are the ones that will make all the difference to how you look and feel on the day.

They might go something like:

1 • I want to have more energy.
2 • I want to feel less bloated.
3 • I want to be a size 12.
4 • I want to have glowing skin.
5 • I want to feel sexy.

Now this list is made up of desires, which are not yet a reality. They will be. And one great way of getting closer to reality is by turning them into statements, in the present tense. So:

1 • I am full of energy.
2 • I never feel bloated.
3 • I'm a stunning size 12.
4 • I have glowing skin.
5 • I feel sexy.

Now your turn:

My Wedding Goals:

1 • _____
2 • _____
3 • _____
4 • _____
5 • _____

You can refer to this list whenever you need extra motivation.

Better still, use them as mantras. You might feel silly at first, but trust me. Look in the mirror, smile and say each statement to your reflection. Believe it. It will soon be your reality.

Practise this, as well as the visualization exercise, every day – or whenever you're experiencing a moment of doubt or stress – to bring your thoughts into focus.

Finally, here's some space to record your measurements and how you look and feel today. At the end of this book, when you've completed the Countdown, you'll do this again. The difference will astound you. That's my promise.

My Vital Statistics, today:

_ _ / _ _ / _ _ _ _

I weigh: _____

Measurements:

bust: _____

waist: _____

hips: _____

thighs: _____

upper arms: _____

My skin is: _____

My hair is: _____

My nails are: _____

Other issues: _____

Today, I feel: _____

A recent photo of myself:

PRINCIPLES OF THE PLAN

The months and weeks leading up to your wedding are an exciting time. Yet for some, they're filled with stress. I don't want you to spend them, as I've seen lots of women do, suffering away under an extreme dieting regime. What you don't want is to be so desperate to slim into your bridal gown, that you'll do anything. Anything is not always best. So hitting the gym for hours on end, day in, day out, and existing on weird and faddy diets is not what I have in mind for you. Would you reach your goal? Maybe. But would you be happy and healthy while you were doing it? Of course not. You would probably walk down the aisle exhausted, uptight and dreaming of doughnuts. A few months after the wedding, you'd be back to square one. So what's different about my Wedding Countdown? Easy. It's NOT A DIET. But before you panic and run back to the book shop for a refund, know this: YOU WILL LOSE WEIGHT.

I do not count calories, or grams of fat, or carbs. You are not going to need a calculator, just commitment. And you know what? You're going to enjoy this. Because I'm going to show you how eating the right foods and ditching the toxic stuff will nourish your body and mind. It's hard to lose weight if you're hungry, tired, moody, bored and craving snacks all the time. Give your body the right fuel and you won't be.

My Promises

If you stick to my Wedding Countdown, the rewards are limitless. You will:

- ❤ Lose weight
- ❤ Reduce cellulite and eliminate bloating
- ❤ Digest food easily
- ❤ Have heaps more energy
- ❤ Cope easily with wedding-planning stress
- ❤ Suffer less from PMS and low moods
- ❤ Be less susceptible to colds and flu, thanks to a bolstered immune system
- ❤ Have a glowing complexion, glossy hair and strong nails
- ❤ Feel more sexy
- ❤ Boost your fertility

Of course, there are countless other serious health and anti-ageing benefits to be had from eating and living well. But what you need to know for your wedding, in short, is this: you will look and feel like a beautiful bride.

But Be Warned . . .

. . . carry on filling up on junk instead of nourishing body, mind and soul with healthy foods and you may:

- ✖ Continue to gain weight
- ✖ Look and feel bloated, flabby and ridden with cellulite
- ✖ Have digestion problems
- ✖ Feel lethargic and incapable of exercise
- ✖ Be stressed, anxious, irritable or depressed
- ✖ Catch every bug going
- ✖ Suffer headaches, allergies, aches and pains
- ✖ Have lacklustre, grey, dry or spotty skin, dull hair and weak nails
- ✖ Lose your sex drive
- ✖ Have fertility problems

You'll also age faster *and* increase your risk of developing serious illnesses, such as diabetes, heart disease and cancers. Is it really worth it?

How the Countdown Works

I've designed this plan to suit every type of bride. Maybe you're super-organized; you finalized the wedding details months ago, and have the next six months to devote to your appearance.

Or, more likely, you're balancing work and family, with hardly enough hours in the day to think about invites and table plans and favours – let alone weight loss. It might even be that you're skipping off to the register office next week, but you'd still like to do what you can between now and then.

Relax. I can help you *all*. Whether you have six months to give me, six weeks or six days, you will see results. All I ask is that you read Part One of this book in full to familiarize yourself with my healthy-eating principles. In an ideal world, you'll read through the whole Countdown, but if time really is of the essence, just skip to the section you need most (weight loss, beauty, vitality or libido). OK, a week's work is never going to result in the profound changes that can occur over several months, but you'd be surprised how much it does do. I have been helping brides-to-be to fit into their wedding dresses for over fifteen years. I know my stuff.

Above all, I know that you're busy, so I've made this simple. You won't find all the complicated 'science bits' and serious health advice that I offer in my other books. There are no meal plans; no difficult menus. You don't have the time and you'd rather be reading bridal magazines than deciphering bewildering day-by-day instructions. I understand completely. So there are just some basic rules to follow, a three-day kick-start detox, some dos and don'ts, plenty of advice, ideas, inspiration and delicious, easy recipes to help you along the way.

Throughout the book, I also answer some of the queries brides have sent me, tackling subjects like beauty, stress and your sex life. Whatever your wedding worry, by the end of this book I will have sorted it for you. Well, apart from your table plan. Sorry, but I'm not doing *that* …

Top ten rules for brides-to-be

1. Eat *more*, not less

This is a diet of abundance. If a food is on my Green list, page 27, you can eat as much of it as you like. I mean it; you can stuff yourself silly. Yes, there are some foods I want you to forget about, but there are lots, lots more I want you to embrace. How many brides have you met who actually ate *more* in the run-up to their wedding? Go for variety too. Every time you go shopping, pick up at least one food you've never tried before. Most people eat the same ten or twelve foods, day in, day out. Not you.

2. Eat *slooowly*

Always take your time over meals. Hands up if you've ever eaten your lunch standing up, from the fridge, not even bothering to put your food on a plate? That stops now. You will sit down and take your time over every meal and every snack. And you will chew and chew and chew until your food becomes liquid.

The digestion process starts in the mouth, where enzymes in your saliva get to work. One of the main causes of digestive disorders is unchewed food.

And poor digestion is not only uncomfortable, it'll have a direct bearing on your looks and health. If you don't digest your food properly you may not absorb all the nutrients it has to offer. You may also suffer problems like bloating, gas, even acne. Who wants a bloated belly on their wedding day? The guests will probably think it's a shotgun wedding!

3. Make your food attractive

Even if you're cooking for yourself, or it's just a snack, present it well. This isn't just to give you a psychological 'I'm not missing out' boost, or appeal to your artistic nature; it's biochemistry. When you see food or smell food, or think about food, the brain sends a message to the salivary glands to start secreting saliva. So, attractive meals actually aid digestion.

4. Eat simply

We normally eat far too many foods at the same meal, making digestion difficult. Some foods are digested more quickly than others, or under different conditions, or require different enzymes.

To make digestion easier and more comfortable, and to maximize weight loss, it's best to eat from no more than two main food groups at each meal.

My food-combining rules in brief: do not eat proteins (that's meat, poultry, cheese, fish, eggs, milk and nuts) at the same time as carbohydrates (grains and grain-based foods, and starchy veg such as potatoes, yams, sweetcorn). You can eat salad or non-starchy veg with either of them. Always eat fruit alone, on an empty stomach, as it is digested much faster than other food.

I am not saying *never* eat proteins and carbs together, but for better digestion, separate them. So many people tell me that my food-combining recommendations have improved their lives dramatically. Look at it like this: it all comes down to the Gas Factor. If you want gas and to look bloated on your wedding day, mix the groups of foods together. If you don't want to bloat and gas, do as I say.

5. Drink water

Most people who come to see me are dehydrated. For good digestion, weight loss, energy, good skin – you name it – the answer is to drink more water. Have up to two litres of water throughout the day – not all in one go. Drink water every hour and you should be OK. Herbal teas count. What you don't want to do is drink your entire day's water quota in one go. Start every day with a cup of warm water, first thing. It goes right through to your bowels and cleans mucus out from the day before. And have a glass 20–25 minutes before meals, not during. Never slug loads of liquids down on top of a meal. That's a recipe for gas.

6. Get the timing right

I want you to eat three meals a day, with snacks in between. Breakfast, snack, lunch, snack, dinner, snack. Don't skip anything.

Most important? Get breakfast under your belt. Never miss it. You are breaking the fast and your body needs fuel for the day. Eating a healthy breakfast will also stabilize your blood-sugar levels, preventing mid-morning energy slumps and cravings.

For the rest of the day, your mantra is 'eat early'. Your main meal wants to be at lunchtime if possible. Late-night eating is a recipe for weight gain. Think about it – you eat a big meal then go to bed. How are you going to burn off those calories?

If you do need to eat late, go easy on your body. Choose from my light-meal choices (page 166) or just have a good snack, or a couple of snacks (page 206).

7. Move it

Exercise is essential for weight loss. I'm not suggesting you embark upon a gruelling, grunting plan which takes you to the sports centre each day. I'm talking about simple, easy movement. The type that will keep your body nimble, supple and young, work off wobbly bits and get you energized. Gentle, daily exercise is great. But anything that makes you break a sweat is even better. (For ideas, see page 97.)

Get into the habit of exercising before you eat. Buy a skipping rope or one of those mini trampolines and bounce around to some music for twenty minutes. This kick-starts your metabolism, and gets your lymph circulating, carrying toxins out.

To reach your goal, you will need to move that bahookee. I require my brides-to-be to exercise for half an hour, three times daily, before all meals. Any exercise you do on top of that is a bonus. You are no exception.

8. Eat fresh and unprocessed

Most so-called convenience foods are processed and/or refined, meaning they've been altered from their natural state. This usually also means they contain fewer nutrients than their fresh, unprocessed counterparts, and often that they're high in nasties like sugar, salt, saturated and trans fats and chemical additives. It's hard, but if you can drastically limit your intake of chemicalized ready meals (there are some healthy ready meals but they are few and far between; check labels), takeaways and pre-packed convenience foods, in favour of fresh ingredients, you'll see and feel the difference.

9. Eat raw

Every time you have something cooked, have something raw with it. Raw fruit, veggies or sprouted grains or seeds are what I call 'living' foods, packed with food enzymes which are our life force. Cooking destroys what are called food enzymes. Enzymes help digestion, metabolism and weight balance and you can only get them from foods that are raw. So if you make soup, for example, add a handful of raw herbs or vegetables as you serve it. If you have a casserole, stew, fish or chicken dish, make sure you have a raw side salad with it or a few raw leaves, herbs or veggies. Most people do not eat nearly enough raw food. You need to make sure you do.

10. Regular 'me' time

When you wake up, the natural tendency for most brides-to-be is to jump out of bed and start running around like a headless chicken. You've got so much to do, I know. But you must not forget about you. The calmer you are during pre-wedding prep, the fewer stress hormones you will release. If you pump out fewer stress hormones, you will reach your weight goal faster and feel a lot better at the same time, especially around the middle. You can end up with a doughnut-type shape and you have not even *looked* at a doughnut. Stress mucks up metabolism and can actually make you fat.

Try this exercise. Sit at the end of the bed and close your eyes. Place your right hand on your tummy and just breathe. Follow the breath. Breathe in through your nose and out through your nose.

With each subsequent breath, try to breathe deeper and longer. Really take your time. You will do the in-and-out nose breathing ten times. Follow this with five in-breaths through the nose and five out-breaths through the mouth. You don't have to visualize at all; don't think about anything, simply follow the breath and do nothing. Most of your day is about do this, do that, do this, do that, pick up this, pick up that, go there, go here, with endless demands and requirements. This five-minute moment of peace with yourself is about doing nothing, allowing your energy to flow freely and letting you simply 'be'. Do my 'me' time every day in the run-up to your wedding day and you will be calmer, happier, stronger, more energized and digesting more optimally. Promise yourself this special time. You deserve it.

Shopping Guide

Red

OK, you'll be shocked when you read some of the following. But I'm not going to apologize. If you want to succeed with the Wedding Countdown, you do not need *any* of the items on this list in your life. So cut them out. Ban them from your cupboards. Skip them in the supermarket. (And no, you can't finish off what you already have at home – bin it now!) Every time you feel one of them calling your name, do your visualization exercise. Is that cake/cocktail/chip really worth it? Of course not. Forgo these foods, even if only until you're married, and you'll thank me for it.

✖ Table salt
✖ Refined white sugar
✖ Processed meats (e.g. sausages, burgers, ham, bacon)
✖ Ready meals unless totally pure and healthy. There are some healthy ones.
✖ Pizzas
✖ Fizzy drinks
✖ Any canned or packaged food with added sugar or salt or other unnecessary additives (check labels)

✖ Cakes and biscuits
✖ Chocolate and sweets
✖ Crisps
✖ Dairy
✖ Caffeine
✖ Alcohol
✖ Hard cheese
✖ Red meat, duck, offal
✖ Pastry products
✖ Ice cream
✖ Refined (white) bread, rice, pasta and noodles
✖ Margarine, butter, lard
✖ Fried food
✖ Mayonnaise, salad dressing (unless it is free of sugar and chemicals), sauces

Top Ten additives to avoid
✖ Acesulfame-K
✖ Artificial colourings
✖ Aspartame
✖ BHA and BHT
✖ Caffeine
✖ Monosodium glutamate (MSG)
✖ Nitrite and nitrate
✖ Potassium bromate
✖ Sulfites
✖ Tartrazine

Amber

These are fine to have once in a while, but moderation is key so don't overdo it.

- ❤ White potatoes (eat white potatoes with lentils)
- ❤ Seafood and shellfish
- ❤ Smoked fish
- ❤ Fresh tuna, marlin, halibut, swordfish
- ❤ Fish canned in oil or tomato sauce
- ❤ Game
- ❤ Goat's milk and cheese
- ❤ Feta
- ❤ Soft cheese
- ❤ Wheat products
- ❤ Certain grains (see also grains in the 'Green' section, below): Basmati rice, brown rice, noodles, corn, couscous, polenta, red and wild rice, rice pasta, risotto rice, semolina, wheat-free pasta, wholemeal pasta
- ❤ Sweeteners – agave syrup, almond extract, apple or grape juice, brown rice syrup, carob amazake, malt extract, mirin, molasses, vanilla extract, honey, maple syrup, no-added-sugar jam

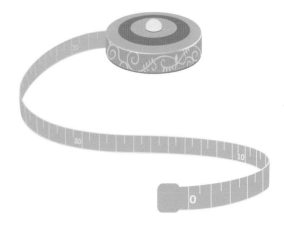

Green

Notice how this list is much longer than the others. You didn't expect that, did you? Most 'diets' or weight-loss plans are all about restriction, but I want you to eat *more*! Boredom is one of the main reasons people quit healthy-eating or slimming plans. They think all there is to eat is brown rice or tiny portions of pre-packed 'diet' foods. Not on my plan. There is so much you can eat you will never get bored. Enjoy!

Fish – choose as fresh as possible, wild rather than farmed. Eat oily fish (mackerel, trout, salmon, sardines, etc.) at least twice a week. White fish (Dover sole, hake, monkfish, sea bass) is also a good source of protein. If you choose canned, make sure it's in water, not brine.

Vegetables – eat fresh, every day. Step out of your comfort zone and try new varieties. Include: brassicas (cabbage, cauliflower, kale); dark green leafy veg (spinach, greens, watercress); root (sweet potato, carrot, parsnip); alliums (onion, leek, garlic); pumpkins and squash; edible stems (asparagus, fennel, kohlrabi).

Sprouts – no, not Brussels, I'm talking about the nutritional powerhouse that is a sprouted seed. Alfalfa, beansprouts, clover . . . all of them. Grow your own! Is that asking too much right now? Well, get hubby to grow them after you are married. That'll keep him busy.

Beans – amazing weight-loss foods. Aduki and mung beans are my top choice. But I also love black, broad, butter, cannellini, flageolet, haricot, kidney and soy beans, black-eyed peas, chickpeas, lentils and split peas. Make stews, casseroles, spreads and dips.

Seeds – flax, raw shelled hemp, poppy, pumpkin, sesame, sunflower, pine nuts

Grains – always choose unrefined (i.e. not white) and remember there's more to life than pasta and rice! Branch out with: amaranth, barley, buckwheat, bulgar wheat, kamut, millet, oats, quinoa, rye, spelt, teff.

Seaweed – agar, arame, kelp, kombu, nori, wakame. Add them to soups, water-stir-fries, salads, sandwiches.

Fruit – oranges are not the only fruit! Fresh is best. Some of my favourites: apples, blackberries, blueberries, goji berries, passion fruit, pomegranates, lemons, mangos, raspberries, watermelon.

Nuts – any, so long as they're raw not roasted, salt-free and sugar-free. I love almonds, hazelnuts, walnuts.

Herbs and spices – great for adding flavour and as salt substitutes. My favourites: basil, chives, mint, parsley, tarragon, allspice, cardamom, cumin, mustard seeds, turmeric.

Condiments – (check out your health-food store) vegetable bouillon, harissa, miso paste, mustard, soya sauce, sugar-free and salt-free tomato sauce, sushi ginger, tahini, tamari, sea salt, umeboshi plum sauce, vinegars (brown rice, cider, red wine, umeboshi, white wine), wasabi.

Good oils – avocado, gold of pleasure seed, hemp, olive, poppy seed, pumpkin, sesame, sunflower, walnut.

Herbal teas – with so many to choose from, you won't miss normal tea or coffee. Try camomile, dandelion, fennel, mint, ginger, lemon balm, rosehip, valerian . . . My all-time favourite? Cleansing, detoxifying nettle.

Chicken and turkey – organic if available.

Eggs – always organic or free-range.

Soya – tofu and tempeh make great meat alternatives, high in protein and calcium.

Yoghurt – natural (live or 'bio' if possible), organic and unsweetened. Try goat's or soya for a change.

Eating Out

I may be a hard taskmistress but I'm not unrealistic. I know that if you're planning your wedding then you won't be in the kitchen all day (unless your husband-to-be is a relic from the 1950s). You'll be out socializing, visiting venues, wedding exhibitions, dress designers. You'll be having hen night(s!), rehearsal dinners. Believe me, I've worked with enough brides to know that in the countdown to your nuptials, you girls don't stop.

Here's how to enjoy eating out, and how to make the right choices when you're grabbing food on the run, so you don't blow it all.

Unfortunately, most of the offerings you'll find in train stations, petrol stations, shopping centres and the like fall into the Red food category. Think crisps, chocolate bars, sweets, biscuits, salted nuts, fizzy cans of drink, mayo-laden white-bread sandwiches . . . You may be hungry but, please, don't give in – you'll only feel just as hungry (and full of regret) half an hour later. The best motto I ever learned from my days as a Girl Guide was 'Be Prepared.' And prepared you must be. If you are a 'Gillian McKeith Bride-To-Be' you would not be caught

dead buying the rubbish on offer at train stations. Take your snacks with you. I don't care if you are planning a wedding, this is my set-in-stone travelling regulation. I would rather you be late for your appointment with a snack in tow, than early with no snack and ready to bite into the first croissant that your potential florist, for example, offers you.

So, keep healthy snacks to hand – in your bag, your car, your desk drawer at work. Bags of nuts or seeds, pieces of fruit or vegetable batons, oatcakes. And don't forget bottled water. Often when we think we're hungry, we're just dehydrated.

Choose independent sandwich shops and cafés over large chains, as the food is more likely to be made to order. That way, you can ask the staff to make your sandwich on rye, hold the mayo, add extra leaves.

Soup is a great option – go for vegetable-based rather than creamy, and skip the croutons or crusty white roll.

Don't be fooled by salad. Make sure it's not covered in greasy, sugary dressing. And if you are opting for salad as a main and not just a side, does it contain a protein, such as chicken or beans? If not, it's not going to keep you full for long. Sushi is low fat and filling, just don't have it every day as the white rice isn't very nutritious (I make my own brown-rice veggie sushi).

In restaurants, keep it simple. Choose grilled and steamed over fried or roasted. Ask for creamy sauces or dressings to be served on the side. If the bread basket is too tempting, ask that it be taken away. In fact, that's my golden rule for restaurants: don't be afraid to ask for it *your* way. A good establishment will always be willing to swap the chips for rice, or offer a healthier alternative. And always remember to stop eating when you're full. They won't make you do the washing-up if you don't clear your plate.

British – beware rich sauces and sugary, overly salty gravies.

Italian – avoid creamy sauces, thick pizza bases and cheesy toppings. Choose the antioxidant-packed tomato-based dishes. Don't go for the pasta and pizzas. Go for minestrone soup, no bread, or avocado and tomato salad, and fish with vegetables and salad.

French – it's hard, but try to avoid the butter and cream. Fill up on veg.

Indian and Thai – mild vegetable curry is your best option. Avoid anything battered or fried. Definitely no naan. Thai 'salads' are a very traditional dish that always feature raw cabbage, carrot and onion topped with steamed fish and dressed with a light spicy dressing of lemon grass, ginger and Kaffir lime leaves. Beware of heavily sugared sauces with Thai cooking.

Chinese – say no to deep-fried *anything* and ask if they can hold the MSG.

Japanese – go get your fill! With miso, tofu, seaweed, vegetables and fish as staples, this is one of the healthiest cuisines around.

Vegetarian – sounds obvious, but choose vegetables and check how they're cooked. Many chefs make up for people's misconception that veggie means tasteless by frying and battering everything, or serving vegetables swimming in dairy or coated with cheese.

A final word on eating out. *Please*, if you're being treated to a romantic dinner or it's a special occasion, don't let guilt spoil it. I will not be sitting on your shoulder like some evil sprite, ticking you off all evening. If you share that lemon tart for dessert, then savour it, and don't spend the next week feeling like a failure. Just remember to get right back on the bridal track the next morning and it'll be our little secret . . . As long as you are doing what I say 90 per cent of the time, you will be fine.

As we are heading towards W day and birthdays are no longer in sight, I do expect 100 per cent commitment. No two ways about it. Period. Over with. Now that we have that little detail sorted out, I need your promise of compliance.

Your Pledge

Do you, _____ [name], promise to stick to my ten rules, to love, honour and obey them, from this day forth, until your wedding day?

'I do.'

Signed _____

Date _____

In return, I promise to be with you every step of the way, from fatter to thinner, from sickness to health! When it comes to looking and feeling fantastic, I'll be your ultimate wedding planner.

Signed

GILLIAN'S THREE-DAY KICK-START DETOX

Why Detox?

If you're new to healthy eating and your diet until now has been pretty poor, a detox will help clear you out and give you a fresh start. It's a good way to kick-start your weight loss too, as it'll get your digestion going and flush out fluid retention, so you'll feel slimmer and more alive in no time at all. The new full-of-life you will be motivated to keep on with the healthy way of life.

Anything that suggests you drastically detox for weeks on end, allows you a very limited range of food, or leaves you starving is a no-no. Steer well clear.

In reality, our bodies are automatically detoxing every day anyway. You shouldn't really need to do anything particularly special, because the body has natural physiological detox actions of its own: sweating, urinating and moving bowels, for example. But modern life is polluted and our digestive systems are often weak, so we sometimes need a helping hand; nothing extreme, just some extra attention to clean eating, drinking and living for a few days.

Excess weight, digestive problems, headaches, bad skin, allergies, bad breath, low moods, insomnia . . . all these and more can be signs that your body is overloaded with toxins, from food and the environment. In my almost two decades of working in private practice with one-to-one consultations with clients, I have found that many symptoms can be reduced by lessening the body's toxic load. Introducing nutritious foods may assist this process for ultimate health. My clients always report a renewed sense of well-being.

And all you brides-to-be have a different starting point: some of you are more nutritionally depleted than others; your food regimes and lifestyles may be OK or not so chipper. So you see, your detox can mean many different things, depending on how you live your life. Detox could mean anything from simply chucking out caffeine to adding more raw food to making veggie juices all day and taking up dancing.

When Should I Detox?

You'll get the best results if you can truly devote time and attention to your detox, so I suggest you spend the three days at home, uninterrupted by chores, appointments or social plans. A quiet long weekend is ideal. If you combine working with detoxing you will end up stressed out, and that defeats the purpose of the detox. Plan ahead so you've got all the supplies you need, tell friends and family you're not to be disturbed (not even for a wedding emergency!), and hole yourself up at home for a relaxing three days of well-being.

I suggest everyone begins my bridal plan with this detox. Whether your goal is weight loss, better skin, whatever, you'll benefit.

And you can always come back to it later on too – if you've let your healthy habits slip, perhaps, and want to get back on track, or if you want to speed up your weight loss.

Detox Treats

I don't want you to look at a detox as any sort of punishment. So banish such thoughts from your mind now! It's a treat for your body and mind, so to ensure that it feels like one, I want you to build lots of pampering and 'me' time (that's *you*, not me!) into your day. Give yourself a manicure, a facial, a hair-conditioning treatment, or why not all three?

One of my favourite pampering treats is a relaxing, sensual bath. Before bed is the perfect time. Dim the lights, fill the bathroom with flickering tea lights, and add about four drops of your favourite essential oil to the bath water. Don't choose anything too stimulating – avoid citrus, rosemary or mint oils. I love frankincense, myrrh, neroli, rose, geranium or lavender. You can add mineral salts to the bath too, for a soothing, deep-relaxation heaven!

SKIN BRUSHING

I always prescribe dry-skin body brushing alongside a detox. But this practice has so many benefits, you brides should be dry-skin brushing daily, never mind waiting for detox days. Do it regularly. Here's how:

Using a long-handled, natural-bristle brush, with fairly stiff bristles, you're going to brush your skin all over while it's still dry. Before your morning shower or evening bath are ideal times.

Brush in long, sweeping movements towards your heart. So from the soles of your feet, up your legs; from your hands to your shoulders. Cover your whole body, being extra gentle on your chest. Avoid varicose or thread veins and broken skin, and don't brush your face.

Dry-skin brushing is a form of manual lymphatic drainage. It stimulates your lymph system, which works alongside your blood circulation and is responsible for carrying toxins out of your body. It also improves skin tone and texture and may help stave off cellulite.

Bride-To-Be Detox

The supplies

- ❤ Dry-skin brush
- ❤ Juicer
- ❤ Blender or food processor
- ❤ Superfood powder to put in your smoothies (optional) – choose from liquid algae, spirulina, wheat grass, my Living
- ❤ Food Energy Powder, chlorella, barley grass. These are all available from your local health-food store
- ❤ Lecithin granules (optional but helpful if you suffer from cellulite)
- ❤ Milk thistle tincture
- ❤ Flaxseeds
- ❤ Candles

Deeper cleansing

For a deeper cleanse, you will need either my 24 Hour Detox sachets, which you can find in health food shops, an enema kit from your local pharmacy or to have a colonic irrigation (bit like an enema except forty times more powerful). This is optional but it is worth the effort.

If you suffer from constipation, get some psyllium husks from the health-food store, please, and follow the directions on the bottle.

The clean-out

'A colonic without the tube' – that's what many people call my 24 Hour Detox sachets.

After many years of working with a large number of women who are desperate to lose weight and brides-to-be who must slide into that dress on their special day, I developed a powder formula to assist detox. My brides-to-be swear by it and tell me that at the last hurdle, my detox helps to knock off a few more pounds – their words, not mine. There's no need to keep weighing yourself to check a few pounds here and there. Forget the weighing, just enjoy the health benefits of the clean-out. And my 24 Hour Detox really does work like a charm. It will give you one of the best clean-outs you have ever had. You will have to stay close to a toilet from 5 p.m. on one evening until 12 noon the next day, as you don't want to get caught out, if you know what I mean. For best results it's also best to combine my 24 Hour Detox with one of the detox days described below, for which meals are planned.

In the raw

My bridal detox focuses on giving you a rich food-enzyme-based regime, which means the inclusion of raw foods – foods that are not cooked. You will help your digestion and have a lot more energy at the end of the three days.

Going raw, or almost all raw, is probably a whole new concept for you but a true gift to your body. You will cook nothing. The food enzymes from raw foods help the digestive process. You will notice that you have more energy when you include more raw food in your life, and an extra plus is that there's no cooking required. In a way, raw food is the healthiest of convenience food. What is easier than peeling a banana and eating it, or washing an apple and biting into it?

Why should I be eating more raw?

Raw foods and salads containing raw vegetables such as tomatoes, carrots, cucumber and celery are great for cleansing the body. They are full of nutrients and enzymes needed by the liver and digestive system. They also nourish the skin, hair and nails.

Green vegetables such as salad leaves, avocado, chicory, fennel and celery provide you with magnesium and B vitamins needed for energy.

Tomatoes contain lycopene that has been shown to have anti-cancer properties. Carrots and squash can be grated to provide beta-carotene needed for healthy lungs, skin and eyes. Beta-carotene helps protect the skin from sun damage. Beetroot can also be grated and is great for building the blood and detoxifying the liver. Salads are also a great way of getting fresh herbs into your diet. Parsley, chervil, basil, coriander, dill, fennel, thyme, mint, oregano and marjoram can all be chopped and sprinkled onto salads. Herbs are high in nutrients as well as flavour. Many are good digestive aids and have anti-bacterial properties.

Having an oil-based dressing on your salad increases the absorption of nutrients from the salad so try using olive, flax or hemp seed oils mixed with lemon juice for extra flavour and nutritional benefits.

Serving suggestion and amounts

Even when you are not doing my three-day detox, I encourage my brides to eat something raw every day. Every time you eat something cooked, there should be some raw food with it. Aim to eat salads at least once a day. Include as wide a variety of vegetables and colours as possible.

NOTE: During each of the three days, make sure you keep up the daily liquid intake of up to two litres. You can achieve this through cups of hot water, herbal teas and veggie juices.

DAY ONE

'Me' time: Start your day with 5 minutes of 'me' time (see page 25). Then drink 1 cup warm water and 1 cup nettle tea – mix 15 drops of milk thistle tincture into your tea.

30-minute exercise: Choose from a gentle walk or skipping or jumping up and down on a mini trampoline.

Dry-skin brush (see page 36 for details on how to do this)

Breakfast: Pineapple Smoothie – blend ½ pineapple with a banana and 120ml water. Sip slowly. Start getting your detox broth prepared (see lunch instructions).

Mid-morning snack: Veggie Juice – juice 6 carrots, 1 celery stick, 1 cucumber, handful parsley and a small piece of ginger (optional). Put superfood powder into your juice, for example ½ teaspoon of spirulina powder.

One-hour gentle walk: Walk for 45–60 minutes in a park. If you have a bike, ride your bike. Rain is no excuse. Take an umbrella. I want you to do this alone. It's about getting close to yourself and spending time with you. If you have a child, see whether you can get someone to babysit for this hour.

Lunch: Detox Broth followed by Chicory and Pea Salad or My Simple Salad.

Detox broth

You will be eating only the broth, not the actual veggies. If you are using organic veggies, you do not need to peel the skin.

2 large potatoes
3 carrots
1 cup red beets
4 celery sticks with leaves
1 cup parsley
1 cup turnips or squash
1 pinch of cayenne
fresh basil for garnish (do not cook)

1. Fill a large saucepan with approximately 2 litres water.
2. Stir the veggies into the water. Bring to the boil, reduce the heat and simmer for 2 hours.
3. Strain the veggies and drink only the broth, which will provide you with a whole load of minerals.

Chicory and pea salad

PREPARATION: 6–8 MINUTES
SERVES 2–3 AS A LIGHT MEAL
OR 4 AS AN ACCOMPANIMENT
2 red or white chicory, trimmed and halved lengthways
2 good handfuls watercress
2 celery sticks, trimmed and sliced
50g mangetout, trimmed
50g fresh peas
50g pine nuts
FOR THE DRESSING:
2 tbsp mild extra virgin olive oil
1 tsp freshly squeezed lemon juice
½ garlic clove, peeled and crushed

1. Toss all the ingredients for the salad together in a medium serving bowl.
2. Whisk the dressing ingredients together with a fork and pour over just before serving.

My simple salad

1 fennel, chopped
1 big handful mangetout
50g raw peas

Toss and serve with a squeeze of lemon and a handful of parsley

Mid-afternoon snack: Veggie juice or some raw veggie crudités, e.g. cucumber, radishes, carrots or fennel, dipped in Olive Tapanade. Although olives are incredibly good for you, there are quite a few people who are not fans. If you are not an olive fan then have Celery Sticks Filled with Cashew Nut Paté instead.

Olive tapanade

100g pitted black olives
2 garlic cloves, peeled and crushed
1 tsp lemon juice

Blend all ingredients until smooth. Place in a jar in fridge and use as and when.

Celery sticks filled with cashew nut pâté

SERVES 2
100g raw cashew nuts
1 tbsp brown rice miso
4 celery sticks, washed

1. Place the cashew nuts and brown rice miso in a small food processor and whizz until smooth.
2. Fill the celery sticks with the pâté and cut into 2cm pieces.

30-minute exercise: Before dinner turn on the radio and dance for 30 minutes.

Dinner: Leftover Broth from lunch and my Sprouting Bean Salad.
This salad serves 3–4 so you can keep some for the next day as a snack or a meal, if you like, or share with your fiancé and friends. If you have plenty of salad from lunchtime, you can always use that instead. But I just want to make sure that you have plenty of choice and ideas.

Sprouting bean salad

SERVES 3–4
125g mixed sprouted pulses, washed
  and drained
1 large carrot, peeled and coarsely grated
4 spring onions, trimmed and sliced
8 baby corn, trimmed and diagonally
  sliced
85g mangetout, trimmed
2 celery sticks, sliced
50g blanched cashew nuts or hazelnuts
  (not roasted or salted)
1 tsp fresh root ginger, finely chopped
FOR THE DRESSING:
3 tbsp cold pressed sunflower oil
2 tsp wheat-free tamari soy sauce
1 tsp toasted sesame oil
1 small garlic clove, peeled and crushed

1. Place the sprouting pulses, carrot, spring onions, baby corn, mangetout, celery, nuts and ginger in a large serving bowl and toss well.

2. Put all the dressing ingredients in a small bowl and stir well. Pour over the salad and toss well together before serving.

TOP TIP

This crunchy salad is packed with raw food energy – it makes a perfect snack, light lunch or accompaniment.

Evening snack: 1 chopped apple

Flax drink: Put 1 tbsp flaxseeds in a mug of warm water and leave to soak overnight. Drink only the broth in the morning.

Bath time: Bathe with mineral salts and lavender essential oil.

Mini meditation: Find a room or place in your house where you will not be disturbed. Place a non-scented white candle safely in front of you. Kick off your shoes or slippers and feel the floor with your feet. Make sure that you are comfortable. You could sit on a chair if it's easier for you.

Light the candle. Close your eyes for a few minutes and place your right hand on your tummy. This area of your body represents your emotional centre. Breathe in through your nose and out through your mouth very slowly five times. Open your eyes and look at the candle flame. The candle flame signifies the burning away of any stress or negative energies you may have collected or created yourself. Continue to breathe deeply in through the nose and out through the mouth.

Notice a sense of relaxation and peace come over your body. Repeat the process for about ten minutes.

Blow out the candle and get to bed. An early night is best.

And congratulations! You have just taken yourself to a whole new level. You have released yourself from the madness of preparations, lists to do this, to do that. It is a rest for the whole of you. Practise this mini meditation on all three evenings of your detox.

DAY TWO

'Me' time: Start your day with 5 minutes of 'me' time. Then drink 1 cup warm water and 1 cup nettle tea or 1 cup dandelion tea, and 1 cup flax broth.

30-minute exercise: Walk

Dry-skin brush

Breakfast: Fruit Salad of apples, pears, nectarines and berries; or a Mango and Berry Smoothie – blend 1 mango and half a dozen strawberries until smooth.

Mid-morning snack: Detox Juice – juice 5 kale leaves, 2 celery sticks, bunch lettuce, juice squeezed from half a lemon, 1 apple, small piece of ginger.

One-hour walk: Go for one-hour walk in the park.

Lunch: Avocado and Cucumber Soup

Avocado and cucumber soup

SERVES 2
2 ripe avocados
1 cucumber, peeled and seeds removed
¼ cup fresh mint leaves
vegetable stock to taste (cold)

1. Place the avocado, cucumber and fresh mint leaves in a processor with a little stock and process until smooth.
2. Add more stock until you have a soup consistency. You can always use a little leftover detox broth as the stock.
3. Serve chilled.

Mid-afternoon snack: Detox Juice, as mid-morning

30-minute exercise: Dance before dinner. Just go crazy.

Dinner: Raw Lasagne with Pesto Sauce

Raw lasagne with pesto sauce

SERVES 2
FOR THE SUN-DRIED TOMATO PASTE:
50g sun-dried tomatoes
warm water
1 tsp tomato puree
1 clove garlic
few drops balsamic vinegar
FOR THE HOMEMADE PESTO:
60g fresh basil leaves
50g pine nuts
1 clove garlic
2 tsp lemon juice
2 tbsps cold water
100ml extra virgin olive oil
FOR THE RAW LASAGNE:
4 courgettes, thinly sliced lengthwise to create sheets
lemon juice
little oil to drizzle

1. Soak the sun-dried tomatoes in warm water for 30 minutes. Transfer to a food processor with 1 tbsp of the water, add the tomato puree, garlic and balsamic vinegar. Process until smooth. Transfer to a small bowl.
2. No need to clean the processor, simply add the pesto ingredients and process again until smooth.
3. Place 4 slices of courgette on 2 plates, add a squeeze of lemon juice and then spread with the tomato paste. Lie 2 further slices of courgettes on top of each lasagne.

4. Add another squeeze of lemon juice and then a layer of pesto, then a further courgette layer. Repeat until you have used all the courgette.

5. Top with a dollop of pesto, garnish with a basil leaf and a drizzle of avocado or olive oil.

Liver lover cocktail: Mix 200ml pink grapefruit juice and 2 tbsp of hemp oil or olive oil together. Add 10 drops of milk thistle tincture (optional but very beneficial). Drink slowly and then lie down on your left side and massage below your right rib for about 5 minutes. Turn onto your right side and rest in that position for another 5 minutes.

Reward yourself with a cup of camomile tea! If anything, it will get rid of the taste in your mouth. You may not find it that bad; everyone is different, with varying degrees of taste receptors. It's a real treat for the liver, though.

Evening snack: 1 peach or pear or apple

Flax drink: Prepare flax drink as on Day One.

Mini meditation (see page 45)

Bath and early to bed

DAY THREE

'Me' time: Start your day with 5 minutes of 'me' time. Then drink 1 cup warm water and 1 cup nettle tea with 15 drops of milk thistle tincture, and 1 cup flax broth.

30-minute exercise: Walk

Dry-skin brush

Breakfast: Large Fruit Smoothie of your choice or a large fruit salad. If you add a superfood powder like my Living Food Energy Powder to your smoothie you will feel fuller and more satisfied for longer.

Mid-morning snack: Veggie Juice

One-hour walk: Walk for an hour in the park.

Lunch: Gazpacho, followed by either Oriental Watercress Salad with Sprouts and Cashew Nuts or Greek-style Vegetables.

Gazpacho

SERVES 2
1 red pepper
2 cloves garlic
300ml fresh tomato juice
½ cucumber, finely diced
1 tsp tamari sauce
2 celery sticks, finely sliced
2 spring onions, finely sliced
lemon juice to taste
2 tbsp fresh parsley, chopped

1. Place the pepper, the peeled garlic cloves, tomato juice and half of the cucumber in the food processor and process until smooth. Add a little tamari to taste.
2. Transfer to a clean container and cover and chill for 2 hours. This is very important for the flavour.
3. Mix the remaining cucumber, celery and spring onion together in a small bowl and add the lemon juice to taste.
4. Spoon the soup into a soup bowl and top with the raw vegetables and parsley before serving. This recipe is enough for two, so save some, if you like, for another day.

Oriental watercress salad with sprouts and cashew nuts

SERVES 2
100g watercress leaves
100g organic alfalfa sprouts
4 spring onions, chopped
50g daikon or radish, finely chopped
120g sugar snap peas
1 red pepper, sliced
100g baby corn
2 tbsp wheat-free tamari
2 tbsp brown rice miso
2 tbsp olive oil
1 large handful cashew nuts

Mix all the ingredients together in a large bowl and serve immediately.

Greek-style vegetables

SERVES 2
2 tbsp olive oil
juice of 2 lemons
1 tsp coriander seeds
2 star anise
2 large tomatoes, cut into wedges
1 red onion, sliced
½ cucumber, roughly chopped
1 fennel, cored and finely sliced
8–10 cos lettuce leaves, roughly torn
2 tbsp pitted black olives
60g firm tofu, cubed
3 tbsp flat leaf parsley, freshly chopped
2 tbsp dill, chopped

1. Place the oil, lemon, stock, coriander seeds and star anise in a screw-top jar, shake well and leave as long as possible to infuse the flavours.
2. Arrange the tomato, onion, cucumber, fennel and lettuce in a serving bowl.
3. Top with the olives, tofu and fresh herbs.
4. Strain the dressing, discarding the seeds and star anise, pour over the salad and serve immediately.

Mid-afternoon snack: Fresh Veggie Juice, as Day One.

30-minute exercise: Dance before dinner.

Dinner: Seaweed Wraps, then, if you fancy rewarding yourself for three fabulous days of detox, go for my delicious Raw Lemon Pudding.
For the seaweed wraps, wasabi paste can be purchased from oriental groceries and health-food shops in small tubes and adds a nice bite to the avocado and chick pea paste. This is an easy recipe and it serves two, so you could save some for tomorrow.

Seaweed wraps

PREPARATION TIME: 10 MINUTES
SERVES 2
2 avocados, peeled and stoned
1 tsp brown rice vinegar
1 300g tin chick peas
wasabi paste
1 tbsp lemon juice
20g toasted nori seaweed sheets (6 pieces)
1 celery stick, peeled and cut into fine strips
½ carrot, peeled and cut into fine strips
½ red pepper, finely sliced
pickled ginger
wheat-free soya sauce

1. Place the avocados, brown rice vinegar, chick peas and a little wasabi paste in the food processor, process for 30 seconds then add the lemon juice and process for a further few seconds.
2. Place a seaweed sheet on a clean working board. Spread a good layer of the avocado mixture over the seaweed. Place a line of celery, carrot, pepper and sprouts down the centre.
3. Carefully roll up the sushi, and roll backwards and forwards a couple of times to tighten the roll. Repeat the process with the remaining ingredients. Place on a plate in the fridge and leave to chill for 5 minutes.
4. Slice the seaweed wraps into 2 cm pieces. Serve with additional wasabi paste, pickled ginger and wheat-free soya sauce to taste.
5. Wrap any unused wraps in cling film and store in the fridge for 1 day.

Gillian's raw lemon pudding

1½ cups lemon flesh
2 cups soft avocado, mashed
2 cups dates, pitted
3 tbsp agave syrup (you may not need
  this, actually)
2 tbsp pear juice
½ lemon, freshly squeezed
½ orange, freshly squeezed

1. Peel lemons with a knife, stripping away the peel and seeds, using only the interior of the lemon flesh.
2. Place all ingredients together and squeeze in the fresh lemon and orange juices. Then mix in a blender or food processor. A fantastic dessert.

Mini meditation

Bath and early to bed

Supercharged Detox
If you want more detox or that final push for your day, then go for a juice and broth/soup day.

1. **Morning:** Fresh Fruit Juice or Fruit Smoothie.
2. **Lunch:** Choose from the Detox Broth (see page 43) or a hot soup or, better yet, a raw soup. Try the following raw soup to get you started.

Tomato Blitz: Place 350g tomatoes, ½ cucumber, handful basil leaves, few drops balsamic vinegar in blender and blitz.

3. **Mid-afternoon and late–afternoon snacks:** Veggie Juice
4. **Dinner:** Veggie Broth or soup and follow that with a crunchy raw cabbage and leafy greens salad.
5. **Evening:** Miso Soup (available in powdered sachets to which you simply add water), or Detox Broth, or crudités of cucumber and celery, or a whole apple.

Help me, Gillian!
I'm worried my hen weekend is going to cancel out all my hard work. My bridesmaid won't tell me what she's organized, but it's bound to be boozy. Shall I go into hiding?
Louise, 27, Surrey

What, and miss out on all the fun? No way. But you can apply some of my damage-limitation tactics.

First of all, I'm assuming the organizer of your hen weekend is a good friend. In which case, it should be in her interests to plan something you will enjoy.

If you've been working hard on my programme, and it sounds like you have, then your bridesmaid must have noticed the change in you. Tell her you're seriously committed to your new lifestyle, and you'd like your hen weekend to reflect that. Say it would be fabulous if she could build some girly pampering into her plans.

Not all hen dos are boozy and unhealthy. Spa days or weekends are a popular and practical alternative that everyone will enjoy. Or what about an adventure day? Mountain bikes and mountaineering aren't just for the boys, you know. And just think how fit you would get!

Tell her you've every intention of letting your hair down and there's nothing to stop you all hitting a nightclub afterwards. Dancing definitely gets the Gillian McKeith seal of approval!

If all these efforts fail, or my advice has come too late and the party's booked, all is not lost. It just takes a little will power. After all, no one can *force* you to choose an unhealthy option on the menu, or the creamiest cocktail, can they?

As a rule, the lighter in colour the alcoholic drink is, the less you'll suffer the next day. And the 'drier' it tastes, the fewer calories it has. So dry white wine or champagne is your best option. But there's no one going to hold a gun to your head and force the alcohol down your throat, is there? You do have choice and you can exercise the right to choose.

However, if you are going to drink, follow this supplement programme to look after your liver – even if you have only a couple of glasses.

Before you go out

❤ Take the homeopathic remedy
Nux Vom
❤ Supplement with 500mg milk thistle
capsule or 30 drops of tincture in a
little water
❤ Artichoke leaf extract will also help
you avoid the morning-after-alcohol ills

The next day

❤ Repeat the dose of Nux Vom
❤ Repeat the dose of milk thistle
❤ Drink 3–6 cups of nettle tea
throughout the day

My Day-after-the-night-before Hangover-recovery Plan

In the event that you do blow it all and
end up bingeing on pina coladas and
alcopops, don't waste too much time
feeling guilty, just get straight on with
my recovery plan.

But be warned: I am only being this
nice because it's your hen do and it's a
special occasion. This is not a get-out
clause for every time you fancy a drink.
It's a one-off.

I realize that if you're away from home
it may be hard to follow my advice to the
letter, but do the best you can.

Whatever you do, don't give in to a
big fry-up. I simply cannot fathom why
people think piling fatty, salty, nutrient-
free foods onto an already stressed liver
is going to make them feel better after a
night on the booze. But for some reason
they do. Greasy foods that are high in
saturated fat, sugar, salt and empty
calories, such as kebabs, are typically
craved after excessive alcohol
consumption because alcohol causes
abrupt blood-sugar highs followed by
troublesome blood-sugar lows, leaving
you starved for energy and nutrients and
looking for a quick fix. Excessive alcohol
consumption also contributes to lowered
levels of the feel-good brain chemical

serotonin, and a kebab binge is the equivalent of self-medicating, to get a fatty, carbohydrate high that *temporarily* boosts serotonin.

Yes, your hunger will be temporarily sated, but just wait until your body starts trying to digest all that rubbish. You will feel awful. TERRIBLE. Don't do it.

Alcohol contains toxins, upsets blood-sugar levels, depletes the body of nutrients and causes dehydration. So, to get over a hangover and undo the damage, you need to support your liver in its work of detoxification, stabilize your blood-sugar levels and replenish lost body fluids and nutrients.

❤ Start with a large glass of warm water with lemon juice to alkalize the body and kick-start your liver and bowel.

❤ To get your blood-sugar levels up eat some fruit or make a smoothie. Berries are great, thanks to their high antioxidant content.

❤ After half an hour or so, breakfast on slow-releasing carbohydrates. Oats are ideal – try a bowl of porridge made with rice milk or oat milk. Sprinkle on some ground seeds rich in EFAs to get your brain functioning again!

❤ Go for a brisk walk in the fresh air to get your circulation going. Staying under the duvet may seem like a nicer option but you'll feel so much better for some oxygen and greenery.

❤ Mid morning, replenish lost minerals and help the liver with a glass of vegetable juice. Try a combination of 1 beetroot, 2 sticks of celery, 2 carrots, and 1 apple with a bit of root ginger. Beetroot is good for the liver, celery is cleansing, carrots provide the antioxidant beta-carotene, apples add sweetness and ginger aids circulation.

❤ Lunch needs to be a large, raw salad. Raw foods contain enzymes and are the richest source of nutrients. Make sure you include sprouted pulses, such as alfalfa, mung beans or lentil sprouts, for energy-giving protein, B vitamins and magnesium. A dressing of olive oil and lemon juice will be good for the liver. If you're really hungry, add a bowl of brown rice or quinoa.

❤ Mid afternoon have either some fruit or another veggie juice. Add some spirulina or blue-green algae for extra benefits.

❤ Half an hour before dinner drink a large glass of warm water and go for another brisk walk or do some stretching.

❤ For dinner, have another large salad, with different ingredients to those you had at lunch to ensure a wide range of nutrients and flavours. Have it with vegetable soup: chop up any vegetables you like; cover with water and simmer for 5–10 minutes; add a teaspoon of miso and blend. Miso contains enzymes that aid digestion and support the beneficial gut bacteria. Sprinkle on some kelp or nori flakes after serving. These are a fantastically rich source of calcium, magnesium, potassium and folate (all depleted by alcohol).

❤ Have an early night and continue to eat lots of fruit and vegetables the next day, with plenty of water and nettle and dandelion teas.

GILLIAN'S No.1 TIP FOR HENS

Once upon a time people held their hen and stag nights on the eve of their wedding. I'd suggest planning yours for *at least* one month before you're due to marry. This will allow you plenty of time to recover, recuperate and get back on track.

THE WEIGHT-LOSS PLAN

Whether it's a few pounds or a few stone, most brides want to lose a bit of weight before they don their gorgeous gowns. Simply following my plan for a new way of eating, outlined in Part One, will help you achieve this. The good news is, it's very hard to stay faithful to my way of living *and* be overweight! I realize, however, that you're probably more keen than most to slim down. And, unlike most people, you have a very specific goal in mind for when you want to see results – your wedding day. *Please* don't weigh yourself. Remember: it's not about the number. Most of all I care about how you feel, how much more energy you will have for your special day; I care that your digestion is better and all your niggly little health sympoms have vanished or diminished. The weight, I can promise you, will take care of itself if you do everything I say to the letter. So let me reassure you – together we will get there. In my experience there is nothing like impending nuptials to spur you on to lose weight. In fact, as a bride, you're my perfect client: you're prepared to listen to me and do exactly what I say. It makes my life easy, really. And your life easier too. What I wouldn't give for more clients like you, I can tell you! Remember that a healthy rate of weight loss is slow and steady (doctors recommend one to two pounds a week). Don't be tempted by fad diets – any regime which delivers instant, remarkable weight loss is not a sustainable one. You will simply lose fluids and perhaps muscle; you will be starving and, in all likelihood, undernourished. The weight will not stay off. Stick with me and you'll see results that *last*. To help you go that extra wedding mile, I am going to tell you all my secrets to rev up your weight-loss efforts. To repeat: simply following my plan is fine. You will lose weight. But in the following pages you'll also find tips and advice, based on my many years of research, that will focus your body on the task at hand. Read on, and you'll find there are foods you can eat, supplements you can take and habits you can get into that will turn you into a weight-loss wonder. Apologies in advance to your poor dressmaker – she's going to be fed up of taking in those seams . . .

Three Foods that Make You Fat

1. 'Bad' Fats

To lose weight, you need to swear off saturated fats. Your body is ill-equipped to deal with these 'bad' fats, found in red or processed meat and dairy products. If you eat them often, raised blood pressure and high cholesterol levels may result. They also play havoc with blood-sugar levels and overload your liver. I am not saying that you can never have a steak again but in the lead-up to the wedding, it's not on the menu. (In the future, your steak, if you have one, should be organic and served with salad and greens.) Cheap sausages and burgers won't be there either.

Even more dangerous to you and a disaster for your waistline are trans fats. You'll see these on food labels as 'hydrogenated' or 'partially hydrogenated' fat or oil. You'll find them in margarine, shortening, crisps, chocolate, sweets, pastries, biscuits, ice cream. Not all of them, granted, but most.

Trans fats have absolutely no nutritional value – *whatsoever*. They will only harm you. Their purpose is to extend the shelf life of food and enhance its flavour – both unnatural processes. Trans fats have been linked with diabetes, heart disease and cancer. They raise bad cholesterol levels as well as depleting stores of good cholesterol.

Your body can't process trans fats effectively. They interfere with metabolism and cause you to gain weight. Eat foods that contain them and they'll literally end up on your hips (and stomach and thighs and bum . . .).

2. Wheat

Here's a typical day's menu for many of my clients: toast for breakfast; sandwich for lunch; pasta for dinner; biscuits for snacks.

Sound familiar? And do you notice anything in common with every single meal? They're *all* wheat based.

We rely far too much on wheat in our diets, particularly refined wheat (in white bread and white pasta). There are other, healthier grains, you know. Wheat is not the slimmer's friend. It contains a sticky substance called gluten that often causes digestive discomfort, particularly bloating, making you look and feel fat. Take a break from wheat and see how much better you feel. Try one of the many gluten-free grain alternatives, such as quinoa or millet.

3. Sugar

When you eat sugar or sugary foods, your blood-sugar levels rise then quickly plummet. It's called a sugar rush. And the inevitable drop leaves you craving more. The more junk you eat – the more sweets, sugary cereals, cakes, biscuits, chocolate, pastries – the more you'll want. The inevitable result of all this overeating? Weight gain. Not to mention mood swings, lethargy, depression and increased risk of disease. But we won't go into all that here (for more on the sugar/energy connection, see 'The Energy Plan', page 96). In terms of weight loss, sugar will make you fat. Period.

Why Digestion is Key

If you've always had trouble losing weight, I'm willing to bet your digestion's not what it should be. Optimum digestion will make such a difference. Poor digestion might cause bloating, flatulence, heartburn, indigestion, constipation or loose bowel movements, IBS and poor nutrient uptake, as well as spots and other skin complaints. One woman on my TV show came to me overweight and suffering from IBS. She had been on the same daily medications for the past twenty years to try to overcome the IBS-related problems, but it seemed to no avail. Three weeks into my food and lifetstyle regime, her IBS symptoms had gone and she no longer needed her medication. And the weight was falling off her.

As well as following my food-combining rules, you'll benefit from taking digestive food enzymes midway through your meals. These are proteins that break down foods into nutrients your body can digest with ease. Find them in supplement form at your health-food store. You'll thank me for it!

If your digestion is sluggish and you're regularly constipated – common in junk-food fans – give it a helping hand with:

- ❤ aloe vera (¼ glass before meals)
- ❤ psyllium husks (1 tsp in water before bed)
- ❤ flaxseeds (soak 1 tbsp overnight in a mug of warm water; drink the broth in the morning)
- ❤ aduki beans
- ❤ nettle tea
- ❤ smoothies

You Can't Lose Weight Without Exercise

Exercise gets your circulation going, transporting all those nutrients around your body. It encourages sweating and keeps your bowels working well, both natural forms of detox. It revs up your metabolism, so you use more calories from fat. It tones muscle so you look leaner and feel stronger. It gives you energy, so the more you do, the more you feel like doing. It can have a positive effect on your libido. It is a natural antidepressant – and it's much easier to love yourself and stick to a healthy-eating programme when you're in a good mood.

Believe me, I have heard all the excuses when it comes to not exercising: you're too busy; you can't afford to join a gym; you hate gyms; you hate team sports; you're too fat to wear Lycra. I'm immune to them all. It's not like I'm asking you to take part in a triathlon or climb Mount Everest. I just want you to get more active on a daily basis. For ideas, see page 97.

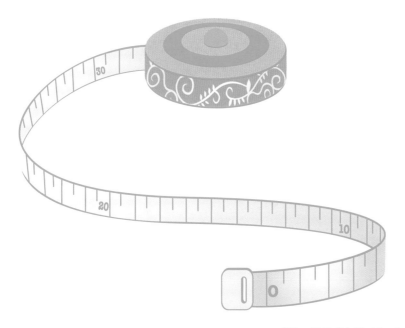

My Essential Tips For Slimming Success

Some other weight-loss must-dos I always share with my clients:

❤ **Get to grips with my food combining.** Find out how in my 'Top Ten Rules' in Part One. I truly believe this is one of the most effective ways to lose and control weight. If you practise this at every meal, you'll optimize your digestion and burn fat more efficiently. You'll also be less likely to suffer indigestion, bloating and gas. My clients notice the difference in days when they food combine my way, and they tell me they feel lighter and more alive.

❤ **Drink eight glasses of water a day.** That's about two litres. Water is a natural appetite suppressant. Have a glass half an hour before meals. If you don't like cold water, drink it warm. In fact, check your tongue in a mirror; if you have a line down the middle or teeth marks round the sides, warm water is better for you than cold. Try to avoid putting ice in your water. Drinks that are overly cold shock the system and can result in bloat and discomfort.

❤ **Get your metabolism going.** Drink a cup of warm water with a squeeze of lemon juice on rising. And then have breakfast – this is the most important meal of the day as it gets your metabolism going. Plus, you have the rest of the day to burn it off.

❤ **Drink nettle tea.** I absolutely *love* nettle tea. It's so good for you. As well as being packed with nutrients (it's a great source of B vits), it supports your metabolism and has diuretic properties which I believe help flush out fat-forming toxins. And it's much more effective than caffeine or sugar for giving you a pick-me-up when you're feeling tired.

❤ **Eat early.** Try not to eat too much, too late at night – if you have a big meal then head off to bed, how do you expect your body to burn it off? Have your main meal at lunchtime if possible.

❤ **Never skip meals.** You might think eating less = weight loss, but not on my plan. If you skip a meal, your brain thinks food is scarce and, ultimately, your body will store more fat in case of famine. Your body is a sophisticated machine, and you can't fool it. Remember my rule: eat more, not less. Embrace snacks.

❤ **Eat the good fats.** These are found in oily fish, nuts and seeds, avocados, vegetables, sprouted seeds. They're all rich in essential fatty acids (EFAs) that get your metabolism going so you'll lose weight and keep it off. That's why I think low-fat or, worse, *no*-fat diets are rubbish. Your body needs fat, just the *right kind*.

❤ **Be prepared.** You stand a much greater chance of succeeding at and enjoying this if you don't put temptation in your way. Make sure your cupboards and fridge are always full of fresh, enticing, colourful foods; your drawer at work is full of nutritious snacks. Don't go shopping when you're hungry.

❤ **Slow down.** Remember what I said in Part One? Sit down to meals, chew your food, put your knife and fork down between mouthfuls, savour the texture and taste. Only by eating slowly will you be able to tell when you're naturally full. It takes twenty minutes from the first mouthful for your brain to signal that you're full. If you wolf down your food in five minutes, you fall prey to 'eyes bigger than stomach' syndrome. You may have wanted only half of what you ate, but you didn't wait to find out!

Can Supplements Help Me Lose Weight?

I am not a fan of caffeine supplements, appetite suppressants, fat metabolizers, fancy pills or potions which claim *solely* to help you lose weight. I'm not saying they won't work, just that if you're following my plan, be sceptical. There are no shortcuts to weight loss and I don't want you to go looking for them. You don't want to rattle down the aisle . . .

However, that said, 90 per cent of overweight people who ask for my help are lacking in nutrients. (I know this because I have these people biochemically tested.) And by getting the right balance of nutrients, weight loss may come much easier to them. This is where supplements *can* help.

I would recommend that you take a daily vitamin B complex supplement in the run-up to your wedding day. The B vitamins are essential for metabolizing carbs and protein, and this is by far the most common deficiency I find in overweight people. If you don't fancy swallowing a capsule, you can open it up and pour the contents into your morning smoothie. You won't taste it, so don't worry. Also the liquid herbal tincture Astragalus (available from health-food stores) is a good source of the all-important Bs and a perfect antidote to

any stress you may feel in the lead- up to your wedding day. Add 15–30 drops daily into your smoothie or even a cup of herbal tea. There's no bad taste; it's actually rather pleasant and a great way to get your B vitamins. After a three-month course of the Bs, either via Astragalus or through a B vitamin supplement, get yourself into the habit of taking a good all-round multivitamin supplement. It's a little bit like an insurance policy, just making sure that you are nutritionally covered, so to speak.

I'd advise taking a green-food supplement too, as an all-round 'great health' insurance policy. Wheatgrass, spirulina and blue-green algae are all dense sources of an amazing range of vitamins, minerals and plant pigments. The latter two also contain enzymes and easily digested protein, supplying all the essential amino acids. I call them superfoods, and incorporating one of them into your daily routine will improve your energy levels, digestion and rate of weight loss. Drink in a little juice or add them to smoothies and soups. You can also try my Living Food Energy Powder. Or why not rotate all of them? Take wheatgrass for a month, then spirulina and so on . . .

YOGA EXERCISE FOR GOOD DIGESTION

I use all kinds of methods to help my brides calm down. And this classic yoga pose has worked wonders for all of them. It releases tension in your solar plexus area, the area from the navel through to the diaphragm, improving digestion and helping to eliminate toxins.

❤ Lie down on your back on the floor (use a blanket or mat if the floor is hard). Relax and take a few moments to unwind, listening to the sound of your breath slowing down.

❤ Bend your knees, sliding your feet up towards your buttocks, as close as you can get them. If you can reach your ankles, hold on to them.

❤ Inhale; then, as you exhale, root your heels into the floor and slowly lift your hips up as high as you can. Only your head, shoulders, upper back and feet will be in contact with the ground.

❤ Stay there for a few breaths and then, as you exhale, slowly roll back down, vertebra by vertebra, until your hips rest on the floor again.

❤ Gently stretch your legs back along the floor and turn your head from side to side.

HOW TO SUPERCHARGE YOUR EFFORTS

As you know by now, I do not advocate crash dieting. So it would be wrong of me to suddenly reveal a secret weapon that means you can double your weight-loss efforts and drop a dress size in a day. Sorry, girls, you're not going to get that kind of crazy talk from me!

What I do have up my sleeve, though, is detoxing. So if you're a latecomer to my programme and your wedding is fast approaching, or if you seem to have reached a slimming plateau and want a little more motivation, you have several options. You can:

❤ do my detox (page 36)
❤ do my detox twice over
❤ do my detox followed by an extra 'juice and broth day' (page 53)
❤ supercharge . . .

The Ultimate Supercharger is Soup

Soup is the ultimate supercharger of weight loss. Have a bowl of soup as an appetizer or a snack, lunch or evening meal. It can be light or hearty. You could even have a soup day. Soup works a treat as it is made up of a hunger-satisfying combination of liquids and solids. Have a day of soups and salads for a change.

The Metabolizers

❤ Ginger can increase metabolism. The volatile oils in ginger work to aid digestion and by so doing they encourage nutrient uptake and weight loss. The Japanese serve ginger slices with sushi to clear the palate and as a digestive aid. Add extra inspiration to your rice side dishes by sprinkling grated ginger, sesame seeds and nori (highly nutritious seaweed) strips on top. Or combine ginger, tamari, olive oil and garlic to make a wonderful salad dressing.

❤ Garlic can give a zap to your metabolic rate, as can many of the gentle spices too. Garlic contains a substance called allicin; this has been shown to give a significant protective quality to cells, which helps to reduce fatty deposits.

❤ Cinnamon improves glucose metabolism, so season with it now and again.

❤ Mustard will raise your metabolism if you add a wee bit of ordinary mustard to the side salad of your meal.

❤ Cayenne pepper not only stimulates the body's metabolic rate, but also cleans fat out of the arteries. You can get cayenne in capsule form at health-food stores.

❤ Any of the warming herbs can help too: basil, coriander, caraway, cumin, dill, fennel, fenugreek, lemon grass, nutmeg, mustard, oregano, spearmint.

Fat-fighting Foods

❤ Almonds! Adding almonds to your diet may contribute to greater satiety and may prevent weight gain. The high levels of fibre and protein could be responsible.

❤ Oats, via their high antioxidant and fibre content, help keep your blood-sugar levels stable. Stable blood sugar is essential for weight loss as it boosts energy and reduces the risk of food cravings. Have oats for breakfast.

❤ Miso soup is a concentrated source of enzymes and nutrients, and also of lecithin, a chemical that breaks down fatty deposits in your body.

❤ Cucumber contains sulphur and silicon, two minerals that work together to stimulate the kidneys. Use half-inch-thick cucumber slices as petite serving 'dishes' for chopped vegetable salads. Or add diced cucumber to tuna or chicken salad recipes.

❤ Apples contain pectin, a fibre that can leave you feeling fuller for longer. Say goodbye to hunger pangs as apples can guard against swings or drops in your blood sugar levels.

❤ Lemon juice or apple cider vinegar in small amounts (1 tbsp) has a powerful decelerating effect on stomach emptying, thereby slowing down the rate of starch digestion. Have a glass of water with lemon in the morning. It's a great way to keep your blood sugar balanced.

❤ Grapefruit is not a diet myth. Grapefruit are loaded with over 15 grams of pectin, which helps curb your appetite by expanding in the body and making you feel fuller, for longer. It is rich in natural galacturonic acid, which adds to the potential to fight fat and cholesterol.

❤ Kelp supplements, or Kombu seaweed, has metabolic precursors of the active hormones of the thyroid gland. It also has naturally occurring iodine in it, which, with the precursors, is believed to increase basal metabolic rate, and help with fat metabolism. Make sure that you eat seaweed three times a week for best slimming effects.

❤ Aduki beans are the beans that I hail as 'My Bean of Weight Loss'. They act in effect like sponges, soaking up excess bloat and damp in the body that can occur when the kidney–adrenal system is out of balance. Adukis strengthen the kidneys and adrenal glands. They are a good source of B vitamins, which are usually sorely depleted in those who are overweight. So if you are wearing more doughnuts than are sold in a doughnut shop, this is the bean for you. NO more than three times a week, mind you, as you might just get a wee bit too thin and dry.

❤ Raw shelled hemp seeds are 'My Seed of Weight Loss'. They are packed with an impressive matrix of metabolic-spurring nutrients and the best ratios of good fats essential for fat metabolism. Make sure you snack on them when you can.

❤ Quinoa and pure protein foods like it have higher than average thermogenic (fat burning) effects.

❤ Fatty fish such as salmon, mackerel and tuna contain Omega 3 fatty acids which can increase the metabolic rate. Other essential fats for a healthy metabolism are Omega 6 fatty acids, especially Gamma Linolenic Acid (GLA). Good sources are evening primrose oil, borage seed oil and blackcurrant oil. If you are not a fish lover, fish oil capsules and flaxseed (either in seed form or as an oil) are great sources of Omega 3 essential fat.

❤ Brussel sprouts, cabbage, broccoli and cauliflower have been shown to improve the functioning of metabolic systems of healthy young people given a diet rich in them. The research showed that all vegetables are good, but the most effective for flushing out the system are broccoli and cauliflower, cabbage and brussel sprouts.

A Slimmer's Menu for Inspiration

As you know, it is one of my mantras that you eat more, not less, so always make sure you eat a good breakfast, lunch, a light meal for dinner and healthy snacks three times a day. See my recipes (pages 117–205) and snack ideas (page 206).

Breakfast
2 grapefruit followed by a bowl of oat bran

Mid-morning snack
Cucumber and celery crudités

Lunch
Beany root vegetable stew (page 153) with steamed cabbage

Mid-afternoon snack
Vegetable juice and/or some raw shelled hemp seeds

Dinner
Big bowl of miso soup or try my Sweet corn and seaweed soup (page 137) with broccoli florets, followed by seaweed salad and crunchy greens with radishes, raw onion, cabbage, pine nuts or walnuts and a squeeze of lemon for dressing

Evening snack
Handful of almonds or a bunch of grapes

Dear Gillian,
I hate gyms, but I need to get rid of my
'bingo-wing' arms before I slip into my
strapless wedding gown. Any tips?
Catherine, 32, Cardiff

Exercise is something you need to build into your life on a regular basis, and slender, elegant arms will come as part of the package if you tone up all over. It's no good doing spot-reduction moves on your arms alone. That said, there are some specific weight-bearing arm exercises you can include in your fitness regime. But I'll tell you about those in a moment.

You say you hate gyms? This is something I hear often from my clients, and I think it's an excuse. They claim the reason they don't exercise is that they find gyms boring, uninspiring places. They may have a point. But to use that as a reason not to exercise at all? Rubbish! What do you think people did before gyms?

Was there a sport you enjoyed at school you could take up again? The possibilities are endless – netball, basketball, hockey, tennis, badminton, squash, women's football, martial arts . . . What about dancing? Ballroom and Latin styles are becoming popular again. Or there's ballet, tap, jazz and belly-dancing. Something I have recently taken up is Hip-Hop and I absolutely love it. You sweat like crazy and get really fit in the process. And there are all manner of ever-changing exercise-class trends (Gliding and Kangaroo Jumps are particularly barmy). Look in your local newspaper, ask at a local leisure centre or do an internet search.

If you're more of a solitary exerciser, try power-walking, jogging, running, cycling. Exercise not only gives you energy, it's also a natural antidepressant and studies have shown that exercising outdoors enhances these effects. It's a great way to appreciate your local environment, to watch the seasons change, and more inspiring than plodding away on a treadmill. If it's a flat, washboard stomach you are looking for, it's got to be Pilates, a toning and strengthening regime that my clients swear by. There are classes all over the country now and once you have learned the mat-work routines, you can do Pilates in the comfort of your own home too. It is one of my favourite ways to keep fit.

Don't forget swimming. It provides a good all-over body workout and breaststroke in particular tones your upper body and arms. Ask at your local baths about swimming lessons. Some pointers on technique and tips for stamina will help you go from a few easy lengths to a proper pool workout.

And climbing is an emerging trend, especially among women, that has the bonus of being great for strengthening your back, shoulders and arms. There are climbing walls opening all over the UK, some in fantastic locations such as old churches. And once you've mastered the technique on a wall, you can start scaling mountains! A personal-trainer friend of mine reckons women have a particular aptitude for mountaineering and climbing. It'll certainly improve your cardiovascular fitness, strength and flexibility. Never mind the sexy arms, you might want to ditch the strapless dress altogether and get married in a bikini!

But back to your bingo wings . . .

For those readers who haven't come across the term, 'bingo wings' refers to those unsightly flaps of flabby skin under your upper arms. Like the abdomen, my personal-trainer friend tells me, chubby upper arms are a real problem area for women, and tricky to fix. And 'wings' are often even more noticeable when you've lost weight.

The muscles in question are your triceps, which run down the back of your upper arm from your shoulder to your elbow. But you'll also need to strengthen your biceps, shoulders, chest and upper back.

The following weight-bearing exercises are effective ways to do just that. If possible, ask a fitness instructor to talk you through each of them to ensure your technique is spot on.

My Top Three Arm-toning Moves

Press-ups

Start off with the easy version.

On all fours, hands directly under your shoulders, exhale as you bend your elbows out to the sides and lower your chest towards the floor. You're aiming to touch your chest down between your hands, keeping your back straight and your abs pulled in. Inhale. As you exhale, raise yourself back to the starting position.

Don't worry if you move barely more than a few inches at first. Persevere and you really will build strength and see progress in a matter of days. Try two sets of 10, building to three sets of 15.

To make it harder, lift and cross your ankles, move your hands forward about 30 cm and lower your hips, so your body is in a straight line from your knees to your head, at 45 degrees to the floor. This is your new start position. All the time, remember to breathe, inhaling and exhaling evenly as you perform your press ups.

Eventually, you can assume the traditional position and do a full press-up.

Triceps Dips

Like the press-up, this exercise uses your own body weight.

Sit right on the edge of a sturdy seat, such as the sofa or a heavy chair – something that's not going to tip up. Put your hands on either side of your hips, on the edge of the seat, fingers facing forward. Your feet are flat on the floor, hip-width apart, a little in front of you.

Pushing down with your hands, lift yourself up and move your bottom forward, so it comes off the edge of the seat. Exhale and use your arms to lower your bottom towards the floor, as far as you can go. Inhale. As you exhale, use your arms to raise yourself back up – not to sitting but so your bottom is just in front of the seat once more.

Aim for two sets of 10, increasing to three sets of 15. You should feel this in your triceps. If not, you're either super-strong already, or you're using your legs. Focus on your triceps as you perform the move.

Biceps curls

This exercise requires some dumb-bells. They're fairly cheap to buy from sports shops (try them out for weight, but 2kg is about right for starters), or you can make do with full cans of food or large water bottles.

Stand up straight, feet hip-width apart. Hold a dumb-bell in each hand, arms by your sides, palms facing inwards, shoulders relaxed. As you exhale, bend your arms at the elbows and raise the dumb-bells towards your shoulders, rotating your forearms as you go so your palms end up facing your shoulders. Inhale. As you exhale, slowly lower your arms back to the starting position.

Try to keep the movement smooth and controlled and your elbows tucked into your waist, not splaying out like chicken wings. Aim for two sets of 10 and work up to three sets of 15. If this is just too easy, you need heavier weights.

GET YOURSELF A FITNESS BUDDY

If motivation is an issue and you're not a natural exerciser, you need a buddy. This is a friend or family member who also wants to get fit, and will commit to doing it with you.

Together, you can make dates to meet up and go for a run, cycle, do a dance class, even stay at home and work out to an aerobics DVD – whatever appeals.

The buddy system is brilliant because if someone else is relying on you to turn up, you won't want to let them down. And on those days when you're feeling unmotivated, you can offer each other encouragement.

You don't have to stick to one buddy, either. Perhaps there'll be a friend you go jogging with on Mondays, a colleague you could do yoga with on Wednesday lunchtimes, and your fiancé to go for country hikes with at the weekends. The more the merrier.

So sign up your mum, your bridesmaid, even your husband-to-be. Let's see who can get fit first!

THE BEAUTY PLAN

Beauty is paramount for brides. And guess what? It starts from the inside. If you're not putting the right, nourishing foods into your body, it'll show. But rest assured that whatever age you are, you can find the beauty within you. **Ready for your close-up?**

Complexion Perfection

When someone says to you, 'You look well!' it's usually a sign that your complexion's at its best – clear, smooth, plump and glowing. And think of how wretched you feel on those mornings when the face in the mirror is tired, grey, haggard, perhaps greasy and pimply or dull and flaky. Makes you feel awful, doesn't it? No amount of make-up on your wedding morning is going to cover up lacklustre skin.

Stick with me and I'll have you looking radiant for your big day.

First up, smokers. Health matters aside, smoking ages your skin like nothing else. I can always tell a smoker; they look like walking corpses. Please, please, quit. A bride with a cigarette in her hand is such a bad look.

Second, water is your skin's very best buddy. If you do nothing else, increase the amount of water you drink to flush toxins out of your system and hydrate your skin cells. Aim for two litres a day. You'll see the difference almost immediately.

And then, of course, your skin needs nutrients. Back in the day when I was a terrible eater, my skin reflected that. Junk food, sugar, saturated fat, chocolate, pastry – you name it, I ate it. A poor diet will manifest itself on your skin one way or another.

So it's back to my Red and Green lists of foods in Part One. To minimize your toxin intake, avoid the Red foods. To maximize your nutrient intake, gorge on the Green ones. Got it? Easy!

There are other factors, of course. Pollution, wind, cold and excess sunlight don't help, so wear a protective moisturizer with an SPF of at least 15. Hormonal fluctuations and stress can also show in your skin, but a good diet will help even these out.

There are some nutrients which are particularly important for skin. When it comes to eliminating waste, for example, you need fibre, from wholegrains, fruit and veg. You can also optimize digestion through food combining (see my 'Top Ten Rules' on page 22).

Fruit and veg also provide you with natural antioxidants, which scavenge on the free-radical molecules in your body that cause premature cell ageing.

While you need to avoid 'bad' saturated and trans fats, essential fatty acids (EFAs), as the name suggests, are a must for plumping up healthy skin. These 'good' fats are found in oily fish, nuts and seeds, avocados, cold-pressed seed oils, dark green leafy veg and wholegrains.

Gillian's Top Ten Skin Foods

1. Water – water and more water. Drink it at room temperature or warm but never with ice.

2. Avocados – rich in the powerful, skin-saving antioxidant vitamin E, as well as wrinkle-busting EFAs

3. Berries – for their antioxidant anthocyanins and collagen-boosting vitamin C. Goji berries get my vote and blueberries are a winner too.

4. Lentils – contain compounds which help repair collagen and elastin for younger-looking skin

5. Grapefruit – keeps you regular but so does nettle tea so don't forget that for your morning starter just before your grapefruit

6. Carrots – a good source of beta-carotene, which helps your body make skin-friendly vitamin A. It may also protect against sun damage.

7. Cruciferous veggies – cabbage, kale, broccoli

8. Oats – contain silicic acid which helps plump skin and reduce lines

9. Brown rice – a top source of fibre, zinc and B vits, for sensitive skin

10. Flaxseeds – for EFAs and digestion

And Five to Ditch

1 ✖ Caffeine
2 ✖ Alcohol
3 ✖ Salt
4 ✖ Red meat
5 ✖ Fried food

Complexion-boosting Supplements

❤ Silica
❤ Zinc
❤ Selenium
❤ Vitamin B complex
❤ Vitamins A, C and E antioxidant formula
❤ Magnesium
❤ Starflower oil (available in capsules from health-food stores)

Be Your Own Facialist

It's vital to consider what you put on your skin, and to keep your chemical load low. Here are my favourite natural skin treats you can make yourself.

❤ A toner helps remove traces of cleanser, refreshes skin and balances skin types. Witch hazel will help clear spots and grease, as will lavender water. Orange flower water is a tonic for normal skins and smells just divine. Rosewater is wonderful for dry or older skins.

❤ Many of the face scrubs you can buy will scratch delicate skin. You'll find much kinder exfoliators in your kitchen. Honey, for example, is brilliant. OK, it's sticky – but that's the point! As you wash it off, it takes with it all the dead skin cells which cause dull skin. Papaya contains enzymes that will literally break down dead skin cells, revealing fresh young skin underneath – mash one up to make a five-minute mask.

❤ Facial massage oxygenates and nourishes skin, giving you a healthy glow – try it and see how much better you look! Massage also helps detoxify skin via lymphatic drainage, and tones facial muscles. Do it as you apply your moisturizer: light, upward strokes on your forehead and neck, circular movements on your cheeks and chin; gently pinch along your eyebrow line, and pat, ever so lightly, around your eye sockets.

❤ Vitamin E oil makes a good anti-oxidant facial moisturizer. If you open a supplement capsule, you'll have just the amount you need for one application.

Other Skin Savers

❤ **Dark circles under your eyes** say three things to me.

1. For heaven's sake get to bed earlier.
2. You may have a food allergy. Rotate the foods you eat and notice when it worsens. Try eliminating wheat.
3. You may have weak kidney energy. Build it up by drinking two glasses of unsweetened cranberry juice every day for a week. Try taking 200mg magnesium, 500mg uva ursi and 500mg horsetail, twice a day. And increase your intake of kidney-nourishing foods: barley, quinoa, garlic, rosehip and dandelion teas, beans, salmon and trout, fennel, onion, beetroot, parsley, berries.

❤ **Little red veins on your cheeks or nose** indicate a lack of digestive enzymes, or that you have been at the booze a bit more than you should. So, the obvious: dump the alcohol and up your intake of raw fruit and veg. Have a dessertspoonful of apple cider vinegar before meals, and take a digestive enzyme supplement halfway through meals.

❤ If you're going to be wearing a sleeveless gown, as most brides do, you don't want **dry, red, pimply arms** spoiling your look. This is a fairly common problem, yet few people realize it can be a sign of nutritional deficiency, and something they can correct. Take 15mg beta-carotene, 50mg vitamin B complex and 1000 starflower oil capsules or a GLA supplement, daily.

❤ For all you need to know about **acne**, and preventing wedding-morning pimple panic, see page 86.

Dear Gillian,
Despite being nearly thirty, I still get acne.
What if I wake up on my wedding day with
a huge pimple on my chin?
Aisha, 29, Glasgow

Nearly every client I've ever seen with acne is deficient in zinc. So before you do anything else, Aisha, make sure you're getting enough of this skin essential.

Zinc is a mineral stored in muscles, bones and skin, and it is needed for protein formation and tissue growth. It reduces inflammation and helps detoxify your body. It's also a powerful antioxidant and helps support immunity and regulate hormones. It can make a huge difference when it comes to your skin.

Up your intake by eating seeds (especially pumpkin and raw shelled hemp seeds), wheatgerm, herring, Brazil nuts, papayas and mangos, and taking a 50mg zinc citrate supplement daily.

We think of spots as a teenage problem, but adult acne is not uncommon. There are all sorts of possible causes, but the usual suspect is a hormone imbalance, which causes the sebaceous glands to produce more oil. If your spots tend to appear on your chin and around your mouth, a hormone imbalance is likely. Try supplementing with the herb agnus castus – particularly if your breakouts are worse at certain times of the month.

Acne is exacerbated by poor elimination (constipation) and poor nutrient uptake. Are you constipated? The skin is one of your major elimination organs, and if you're backed up down below, those toxins will try to escape through your skin, causing breakouts. The majority of my clients who have sluggish bowels also have spotty skin. See 'The Weight-Loss Plan' in Part Two (page 58) for advice on optimizing your digestion.

A healthy, balanced diet will go a long way towards rectifying all these causes, so you can rest assured that by giving my programme your all, you're already well on the way to clearing up your complexion.

Good hydration is crucial too. It helps flush toxins out of the body, improves digestion and keeps skin cells hydrated and young. Make sure you're drinking two litres of water a day. This can include juices and herbal teas, and I'd urge you to start drinking nettle and dandelion teas, great for detoxification and clear skin.

It's extra important to avoid all the food nasties (on my Red list). Sugar, refined foods, saturated fats and alcohol all trigger breakouts; they're toxins for your insides so they show on the outside. Dairy is a common trigger too.

Instead, eat plenty of fresh fruit and veg and raw vegetable juices – carrot, lettuce, nettle, watercress, celery and dandelion are all great cleansers. Eat seaweeds such as kombu and wakame. They have a cooling effect on the blood and I've always found them useful for acne. The herb Agnus Cantus is useful too.

Finally, people tend to equate eating fats with oily skin, but this is not true of essential fatty acids (EFAs). You need EFAs for healthy, hydrated skin and they're particularly useful for acne as they reduce inflammation and help balance hormones. So ensure your diet includes plenty of oily fish, seeds and dark green leafy vegetables.

Whatever's going on under your skin to make it greasy and inflamed, there are many external factors which can contribute, such as pollution, smoking, make-up, using phones, touching your face and transferring germs. Get into the habit of cleansing your face as soon as you get home. Never, ever sleep in your make-up. Try using witch hazel or lavender water as a post-cleansing toner – both great for balancing oily skin.

Skin-friendly recipes to try:
- ❤ Raw shelled hemp seeds mashed into a baked sweet potato
- ❤ Avocado, tomato and basil salad
- ❤ Baked salmon parcels (page 156)
- ❤ Watercress soup (page 141)
- ❤ Fruit smoothies
- ❤ Brown rice seaweed salad (page 168)

Skin Declogger and Cleanser

Try an old herbal remedy of lavender with apple cider vinegar. Mix lavender flower heads in 1 litre of apple cider vinegar. Leave for a while and then strain. For every tablespoon of lavender/apple cider vinegar liquid, add 125ml water. You can use this declogger liquid as your facial cleanser.

My Anti-acne Supplement Plan

Zinc – 50mg daily
Vitamin C – 1000mg daily
Beta-carotene – 25,000iu daily (do not take if pregnant)
B complex – 50mg twice daily
Digestive enzyme supplements – take midway through meals to improve digestion and nutrient uptake
Flaxseed oil – 2 tbsps daily, or starflower oil – 1000mg daily
Probiotics – to ensure good gut health and prevent yeast overgrowth, another cause of breakouts. Try a powdered acidophilus supplement.
Tissue cell salts – silicea or silica can really help clear the skin of impurities.

Crisis Management

If, despite all your efforts, the worst happens and a pesky pimple erupts just before your big day, don't panic.

Brides – in fact, make that women in general – have an inbuilt magnifying glass when they look in the mirror. It zones in on every possible blemish, making you see it as twice the size, twice as red and twice as visible as it really is. Chances are, no one else will even notice it.

Under any normal circumstances I would insist you leave well alone. Touching spots just spreads bacteria and inflammation, making the situation worse.

However, I understand that these are exceptional circumstances. So here's my emergency action plan:

1. First, wash your hands. Don't just show them to the tap – give them a thorough cleanse and scrub under your nails.

2. Next, if – and only if – the offending blemish has a very prominent white or yellow head, you may squeeze it. But in the right way. Take a sharp sewing needle and sterilize it using a disinfectant such as surgical spirit. Dab a little on the pimple too. Then use the needle to make a small hole in the centre of the pimple.

3. Very, very gently squeeze the spot so all the pus comes out – but not so much you tear the skin or make it bleed, or it won't stop.

4. Wipe the area with some witch hazel. You can also take an ice cube, wrap it in a clean hankie that you've dipped in witch hazel, and use this as a cold compress to apply to the spot to bring the inflammation down.

5. Apply some diluted hydrogen peroxide – or, my preference, tea tree or lavender essential oil – to the blemish. Both these oils have antibacterial and healing properties and will send your pimple packing, fast.

If your spot has not formed a head, whatever you do, do NOT squeeze it. You will only make the surrounding area red and angry and make the spot much, much worse. Instead, follow instructions number 1, 4 and 5 above.

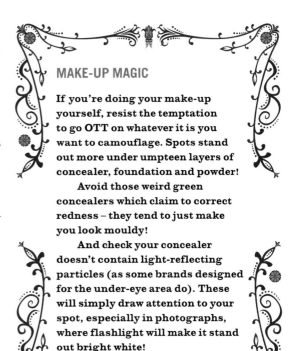

MAKE-UP MAGIC

If you're doing your make-up yourself, resist the temptation to go OTT on whatever it is you want to camouflage. Spots stand out more under umpteen layers of concealer, foundation and powder!

Avoid those weird green concealers which claim to correct redness – they tend to just make you look mouldy!

And check your concealer doesn't contain light-reflecting particles (as some brands designed for the under-eye area do). These will simply draw attention to your spot, especially in photographs, where flashlight will make it stand out bright white!

Cellulite – Busted

Some insist that cellulite does not exist. Try telling that to any woman who has that distinctive lumpy, bumpy orange peel on her hips, bum and thighs!

Cellulite is caused by clumps of unmetabolized fat, water and waste, trapped beneath connective skin tissues. It hardens, resulting in those unsightly lumps. What causes it? Oestrogen imbalance, poor circulation and, most importantly, an overworked liver. Follow this advice and your honeymoon bikini body will never have looked better.

❤ Alcohol and caffeine cause cellulite. I promise you. If you haven't already cut them out 100 per cent, quit now.

❤ Nettle tea is my all-time favourite detoxing drink. It's a natural diuretic, so it'll help flush out excess fluids and toxins. As well as plenty of water, drink three cups of this a day.

❤ Reduce salt to prevent fluid retention and cellulite – use herbs instead.

❤ Help your liver do its job by taking a daily milk thistle supplement – 30 drops in a glass of water.

❤ The herb agnus castus may help balance female hormone levels.

❤ Eat more fruit and veg, especially berries and cruciferous veggies.

❤ You've got to exercise. Full stop. It boosts circulation and the more muscle mass you have, the less fat you'll carry, so the less cellulite. Simple.

❤ Dry-skin body brushing (see my 'Three-day Detox', page 38) prompts toxin elimination and is a form of toning self-massage. It sloughs off dead skin for a smoother appearance and feel.

❤ Make your own cellulite-zapping body scrub to massage into wet skin in the shower. Mix together olive oil with sea salt, to a consistency you like. Add up to 10 drops of detoxifying juniper essential oil. Grab a handful and get rubbing!

Your Crowning Glory

Hairdressers will tell you that using harsh chemicals and heated appliances damages hair. True. But the condition of your locks reveals as much about your well-being as it does about your styling habits.

Hair is made up of a protein called keratin. So you need to eat plenty of protein to ensure a glossy mane. Good sources are beans, seeds and fish. You'll also need a healthy spectrum of minerals, and for this you can't beat seaweeds. Add them to soups, salads, stir-fries and stews. A great source of both protein and minerals is blue-green algae (see 'Nail it', below).

Essential Fatty Acids (EFAs) help keep your scalp moisturized, so don't miss out on oily fish, nuts and seeds. Silica is vital for strong, lustrous hair. Find it in onions, garlic, green leafy veg and sprouted seeds.

If you want to grow your hair for your wedding, you'll need strong kidneys. Sounds barmy, but there's a connection. So be kind to your kidneys by cutting down on salt and processed foods, and by getting enough water and kidney-nourishing foods (see 'Dark circles under your eyes', above).

Troubleshooting Hair Tips

❤ **Don't let dandruff get a look in** – confetti is the only thing you want scattered over your shoulders in the photos. You're probably deficient in EFAs, so have two dessertspoonfuls of flaxseed oil a day (or you can take it in supplement form). Eat a few Brazil nuts daily too, for their high selenium content. Sugary foods are a real no-no. It's possible too that there's an overgrowth of intestinal yeast. So you can take a Biotin supplement to help prevent yeasts budding full cycle, and drink Pau D'Arco tea. If it's really bad, go on a short course of a supplement called Caprylic Acid. Beneficial bacterias and green superfoods will help too, and you can get all of these in the health-food store.

❤ **Healthy hair needs good circulation** to the scalp, particularly if you're growing it. Before every wash, give your head a thorough massage –like a dry shampoo. Hang your head upside down to boost the blood flow even more, bringing oxygen and nutrients to the area. Then brush your hair to distribute the natural hair oils you've just loosened.

❤ **Avoid chemicals.** Just as I advise you to steer clear of unnatural chemical additives in food, so I think it's best to choose natural, organic beauty products. Shampoos, for example, often contain harsh chemical detergents – they're one step away from washing-up liquid! Chemicals can be irritating and many are able to penetrate into your body. Seek out natural shampoos with ingredients such as dead sea minerals, aloe vera, tea tree oil or nettle.

Natural DIY Hair Treats

❤ A conditioning mask that's good enough to eat – Mash up one ripe avocado with 1 tbsp olive oil. Rub into your hair and scalp, pop on a shower cap, leave for half an hour, then shampoo out.

❤ An egg-cellent shampoo – Beat an egg and use it in place of shampoo. It'll make your hair super shiny!

❤ The acid test – For centuries, women have used vinegar as a final rinse after shampooing. It helps neutralize the effects of alkaline shampoo, and is great for oily *or* dry hair, and dandruff. Apple cider vinegar is the best. Use half a cup mixed with one cup of water for glossy, tangle-free hair.

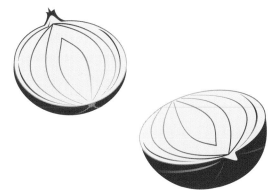

Nail It

When your fiancé slips that band of gold onto your finger, you want an elegant manicure to show it off. I always check the state of people's fingernails – and I don't just mean whether or not they've cleaned under them! It doesn't matter whether you like yours long or short, painted or *au naturel* – healthy nails should be strong, flexible and pink, with no ridges, dents, white marks or hang nails. If they're not, something's out of kilter with your health.

That's because nails are made up of a protein (keratin, like your hair) and minerals including calcium, sulphur, potassium and selenium. Ensure adequate amounts of these in your diet by taking a blue-green algae supplement such as spirulina – rich in digestible protein, minerals, beta-carotene and EFAs. Buy it in tablet form or as powder to add to smoothies and juices.

Troubleshooting Nail Tips

❤ **White marks?** Snack on zinc-rich pumpkin, sunflower and raw shelled hemp seeds.

❤ **If your nails are prone to breaking, splitting or flaking**, your liver may need support. Take the herb milk thistle daily, in capsule or tincture form, and drink nettle tea. You may also be low in digestive enzyme function so take Betaine with HCL *before* meals for a month or so.

❤ **For strong nails**, calcium is essential. Eat plenty of dark green leafy veg and try the herbal supplement horsetail. This contains calcium and silica, a mineral that helps calcium absorption. The greens are important for their magnesium too, as magnesium mobilizes calcium.

Natural DIY Nail Treats

❤ Rub sweet almond oil into your cuticles every day. Your cuticles protect the nail bed and if you keep them moisturized and nourished, you'll be surprised how much it improves the condition and appearance of your nails.

❤ Make an exfoliating and moisturizing hand scrub by mixing a handful of oats with a dessertspoonful of olive oil or gold of pleasure seed oil. Massage well into your hands, rinse off the oats and pat dry. The oil will keep your hands smooth and supple.

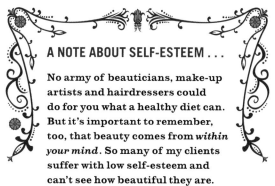

A NOTE ABOUT SELF-ESTEEM . . .

No army of beauticians, make-up artists and hairdressers could do for you what a healthy diet can. But it's important to remember, too, that beauty comes from *within your mind*. So many of my clients suffer with low self-esteem and can't see how beautiful they are.

It's hard to feel attractive when you're overweight, unfit and unhappy. But now you know you're working on all those things, it's time to start looking at yourself differently.

Every morning when you wake and every night before bed, I want you to look at yourself in the mirror, smile, and say: 'I am beautiful'. It doesn't matter if you laugh – or cringe – at first. Repeat this exercise every day and, eventually, you'll believe it.

And for moments when your self-image is floundering, add two drops of the Bach Flower Remedy Crab Apple to a glass of water, and sip it slowly.

Eat Yourself Beautiful

Start the day with a large glass of warm water followed by a mug of rosehip tea.

Breakfast
Nectarine berry boost smoothie (page 130) followed by Barley flake porridge (page 120) with 1 tbsp of ground flaxseeds

Mid-morning snack
Large vegetable juice made from 2 celery sticks, a couple of chard leaves, ½ a fennel and 2 apples; or kale, lettuce, celery, lemon

Lunch
Soup of choice with Red warmer lentil salad (page 181)

Mid-afternoon snack
Half a cup of berries or a pear

Dinner
Baked salmon parcels (page 156) with a generous side salad

Evening snack
Mash avocado into a baked sweet potato with vegetable crudités of cucumber, celery and fennel

THE ENERGY PLAN

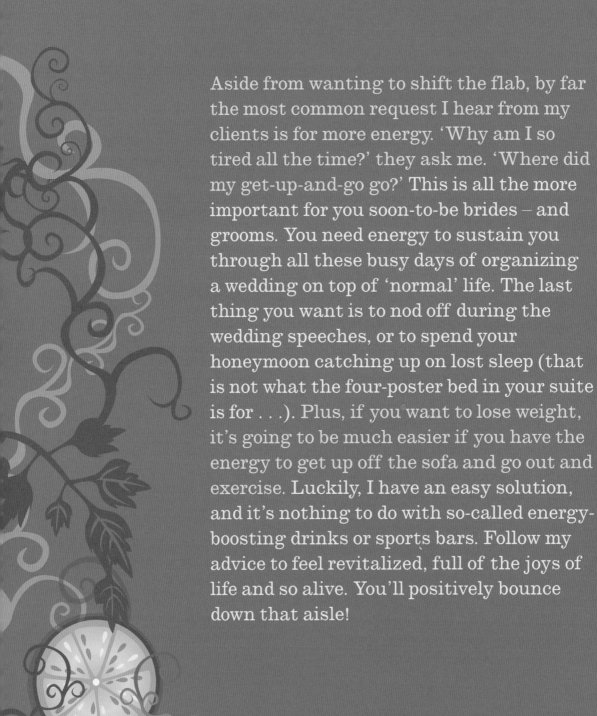

Aside from wanting to shift the flab, by far the most common request I hear from my clients is for more energy. 'Why am I so tired all the time?' they ask me. 'Where did my get-up-and-go go?' This is all the more important for you soon-to-be brides – and grooms. You need energy to sustain you through all these busy days of organizing a wedding on top of 'normal' life. The last thing you want is to nod off during the wedding speeches, or to spend your honeymoon catching up on lost sleep (that is not what the four-poster bed in your suite is for . . .). Plus, if you want to lose weight, it's going to be much easier if you have the energy to get up off the sofa and go out and exercise. Luckily, I have an easy solution, and it's nothing to do with so-called energy-boosting drinks or sports bars. Follow my advice to feel revitalized, full of the joys of life and so alive. You'll positively bounce down that aisle!

Three Reasons You're Tired All the Time

1. You need to exercise more

Have you heard about the energy paradox? You think you're too tired to do it, but exercise actually *gives you energy*. I really have to hammer this home to people because they don't believe me. 'Try it right now,' I tell them. 'Get up, go out for a brisk walk for twenty minutes. You'll feel more awake and energized after your walk, I absolutely guarantee it.'

If you're not the fitness type, start off just by building more movement into your day. Leave the car at home for short journeys and walk instead. If you work in an office, don't eat your lunch at your desk – get off your butt and run some errands that involve a healthy stroll. Promise yourself you will ignore lifts and escalators in favour of the stairs. Every time you think, 'I'm too knackered for this,' remind yourself of the energy paradox.

It goes without saying that you need to sleep well for energy too, and exercise will certainly help this. (For more on getting a good night's slumber, see Part Three.)

2. Your blood-sugar levels are going crazy

Your body needs sugar (glucose) for energy, and it gets most of this from carbohydrates. When sugar enters your bloodstream, your pancreas releases insulin, which takes the sugar to be stored in your liver and muscles.

However, some foods – namely refined, processed ones like white bread, white pasta and rice, cakes, sweets, sugary foods and drinks – cause blood-sugar levels to rise unnaturally fast. This means that a large amount of glucose goes into the bloodstream in too short a space of time. These foods are so low in nutrients that they behave like pure sugar when they enter your blood. In response to this peak, your pancreas releases too much insulin, which takes your blood-sugar levels down too low. Still with me?

Good. What this means, in easy terms, is that when you eat the wrong food, you get an instant energy fix but pretty soon you feel lousy again. Try it for yourself: have a big, gooey Danish pastry for breakfast, washed down with a sugary coffee, and time how long it takes before you're tired, irritable and craving something else to eat.

To get the reverse effects, stay away from the food nasties and eat 'good' complex carbohydrates instead – particularly wholegrains and vegetables. These are not stripped of their nutrients like their refined counterparts, and are able to be metabolized *slowly* by your body, for sustained energy release. Complex carbs will keep you fuller, your energy higher and your mood better, for longer.

As well as food choices, good eating habits help stabilize energy levels. Always, *always* eat breakfast – porridge is the perfect choice. Food combine at mealtimes (see my 'Top Ten Rules' in Part One), and don't forget snacks.

If you're used to putting yourself on faddy, restrictive diets, you may have a bad relationship with snacking. I'm here to tell you that snacking is *good*. It keeps blood sugar balanced and stops you giving in to cravings. Three meals a day is not enough, so no more depriving yourself. Keep fruit, raw veg, nuts, seeds and oatcakes handy for mid-morning and afternoon snacks.

Finally, I know your first thought when you need a pick-me-up is probably to make a cuppa, open a can of cola or pop by the coffee shop for an espresso. Believe me, this is counterproductive. Caffeine is a stimulant. It causes your blood pressure and sugar to rise rapidly so, sure, you feel more alert at first. But it rapidly wears off, levels plummet and you'll feel even worse – tired, moody, headachy, anxious. Caffeine contains the chemical benzoic acid. This is essentially toxic and your body has to neutralize its negative effects with an amino acid called glycine. But glycine is supposed to build up and repair collagen, which keeps the skin firm and wrinkle free. But if your glycine stores are used up just from your coffee drinking, where does that leave your skin? Caffeine also exhausts your adrenal glands, making you stressed and knackered and, if you drink lots of it, it can dehydrate you. Dehydration is a *major* cause of tiredness. If you're yawning during the day, it could be your body saying, 'Glass of water, please!' (If you are really struggling to come off coffee, try dandelion coffee as an alternative. My brides tell me that it helps to wean them off their old coffee fix. It is good for your liver and has no caffeine. You will need to get yourself down to the health-food store to get some shop but it's worth it.)

3. You need these nutrients

A healthy, balanced diet will include all the nutrients you need. But, depending on the strength of your digestive system, your ability to assimilate nutrients from food, the quality of your food and your starting point, and if you need to give yourself an energy boost, you should focus on getting plenty of the following, which are essential for energy production:

B vitamins – B deficiency may cause poor adrenal gland function, which leads to energy lows. Find B vitamins in wholegrains, beans, green leafy veg, seaweed, seeds, oats, nettle tea.

Magnesium – vital for enzyme function. Found in grapes, nuts, wholegrains, fish and dark green leafy vegetables.

Co-enzyme Q10 – increases oxygen uptake in all your cells, raising energy levels. Find it in sardines, broccoli, sesame seeds, lean white meats.

Iron – tiredness is a chief sign of iron deficiency. Ensure good levels with beans, dark green leafy veg such as kale and watercress, sunflower seeds, unsulphured dried fruit. The herb Yellow Dock can help Iron absorbption. Drink Nettle tea too.

Vitamin C – helps boost metabolism. Get yours from parsley, peppers, yams and squashes, berries, broccoli, seaweed.

Gillian's Top Ten Energy-boosting Foods

1 ❧ Nettle tea
2 ❧ Sunflower seeds
3 ❧ Goji berries
4 ❧ Wholegrains such as brown rice, oats and quinoa
5 ❧ Mung beans
6 ❧ Blueberries
7 ❧ Peaches
8 ❧ Broccoli
9 ❧ Spinach
10 ❧ Sprouted seeds and sprouted grains

And Five to Avoid

1 ✖ Sugary foods
2 ✖ Fizzy drinks
3 ✖ Salty, fatty foods
4 ✖ Alcohol
5 ✖ Caffeine

Energy-boosting Supplements

Vitamin B complex – your energy and mood essential
Co-enzyme Q10 – exhaustion is its enemy
Siberian ginseng – may improve physical and mental energy, especially during times of stress, as it helps you adapt to stressors. Wedding planning can bring plenty of those.
Ginkgo biloba – boosts oxygen supply to your brain, making you feel more 'with it'
Magnesium – I have found that of the brides-to-be who come to see me for the first time more than 85 per cent test deficient in what I call the energy mineral. Magnesium is the catalyst for at least seventy-eight different enzyme reactions in the body.
Chromium – works with insulin to control blood sugar. Take with your lunch to reduce mid-afternoon cravings.
Astragalus – used in Chinese medicine for a natural energy lift
Living Food Energy Powder – my own formula. Does exactly what it says on the bottle!

Gillian's Sweet Treats to Curb Cravings

No need to answer the chocolate bar that's calling your name – try one of these instead:

❤ Fresh, bite-sized fruit – grapes, strawberries, blueberries

❤ Fresh fruit smoothies

❤ Dried figs, dates and prunes

❤ Natural, organic yoghurt with no added sugar or sweeteners

❤ Oatcake spread with no-added-sugar jam

❤ Cacao bits – the antioxidant-rich cocoa bean by itself, without all the sugar and additive rubbish which, when added, makes the cacao bean into chocolate

❤ Date truffles – blended dates rolled in carob powder

❤ Cacao smoothie: blend 1 banana, 120ml rice milk or water with 1 tbsp cacao powder. Cacao contains B vitamins which can influence the neourotransmitter anandamide, known as the the 'bliss chemical'. Cacao is one of the richest sources of magnesium, so this blissful smoothie should put you into a good mood.

❤ My rice pudding. All you have to do is simmer 1 part brown rice with 3 parts rice milk along with 1 cinnamon stick and the juice of 1 lemon for 30–40 minutes. Comfort eating suddenly has a whole new healthy meaning.

GILLIAN SAYS . . .

If you feel more exhausted than normal, for more than a fortnight, and none of these measures work, you must see your GP to rule out medical causes.

Round-the-clock Energy Menu

Start the day with a cup of warm water followed
by a cup of nettle tea

Breakfast
Banana, peach and raspberry smoothie followed
by oat porridge

Mid-morning snack
Apple, carrot and beetroot juice with ginger.
Add 1 teaspoon of Living Foods Energy Powder
or spirulina for an extra boost

Lunch
Aduki bean and corn broth with avocado (page 132)

Mid-afternoon snack
Sunflower seeds or a handful of hazelnuts

Dinner
Salmon and savoy cabbage 'lasagne' (page 159)

Evening snack
Handful of soaked almonds

**Dear Gillian,
Is planning a wedding supposed to be *this* stressful? My fiancé and I keep snapping at each other, and if I see another table plan I'll scream!
Frances, 26, Belfast**

Planning a wedding should be a whirlwind of excitement and anticipation of fun to come. But what with managing a budget, booking the venue, hunting for dresses, sorting the flowers, trying to satisfy all members of both your families – *and* holding down a job and home life – it's often a big source of stress. I know of brides who have become so uptight that they have come out in hives. That's the last thing you want for your wedding day. So take a deep breath and follow my advice.

Every bride's situation is different. Whether or not you give in to your mother's wishes and invite all your second and third cousins twice-removed, for example, may depend on who's financing your wedding. Striking the balance between having the day you desire and not causing a family rift (or debts) is difficult, and you won't be the first couple to feel the pressure. Even if budgets and family harmony are not issues, there's still so much to do (unless you're one of the fortunate few who has a wedding planner). It's a once-in-a-lifetime occasion so you want everything to be perfect. But this is where some girls start to lose perspective and turn into 'bridezillas'.

All too many couples get so carried away with creating their perfect day that what really counts, their relationship, gets forgotten. And before you know it, that man waiting for you at the end of the aisle is like a stranger.

What I want you to do – starting today – is commit to having one 'wedding-free' day a week, when you and he aren't allowed to even mention it, your future mother-in-law's not allowed to call and discuss the flowers, the dress fitting can wait.

Instead, have a date with your partner. Take it in turns to plan something special, be it a meal out or a long soak together in a bubble bath.

Exercise is another proven stress-buster. So rope hubby-to-be in on this one too. Play tennis together or go out dancing. And remember that wedding talk is still off the agenda.

In those moments when you feel the anxiety rising, try to get outside into the fresh air and take a brisk walk. Breathe slowly and deeply and feel the panic subside. As you exhale, say the word 'calm' quietly to yourself, and you soon will be.

And the next time you and your Mr Right start sighing or snapping at each other? Head straight for the bedroom – sex is one of the best stress-relievers there is (turn to page 108 for tips on how to lift your libido). And after a stress-relieving sexy session with your man, you can get a good night's sleep.

During sleep your adrenal glands are restored and repaired. Remember that your adrenal glands are your front line when it comes to coping with stress. Eat lots of vitamin B rich brown rice and quinoa, and you could also start taking a vitamin B complex. Unfortunately, most of us place little value on sleep, and end up getting less than we need, night after night. Result: your adrenal glands stay depleted and you get stressed. The average person needs eight hours of sleep each night.

Eat Yourself Calm

The right foods will definitely help you to handle stress. The wrong ones will intensify all its effects and even add to them. So keeping your diet on track through potentially stressful periods is a wise move, and could just make planning your wedding a more pleasant experience.

Overproduction of stress hormones can lead to adrenal exhaustion (see 'What happens to your body when you're stressed?', below). And that's when your ability to cope plummets.

Caffeine and alcohol, ironically, are stimulants people often turn to when they're stressed – a strong coffee to get them through that long work meeting, a stronger G&T to unwind at the end of the day. But they both have the reverse effect, stimulating adrenalin, increasing stress and limiting your liver's ability to detoxify your body properly.

Sugar and salty foods may also deplete your adrenal gland, while fatty foods, dairy, red meat and processed foods will put unnecessary strain on your digestion and fail your body when it needs all the nourishment it can get.

What you need to do is nourish your body with foods that support adrenal function.

Foods rich in the B vitamins, zinc and magnesium are particularly important, as are a good range of antioxidants (vitamins A, C, E and selenium) and foods which support the liver and aid detoxification. The following are great to eat on a regular basis.

Gillian's Top Ten Anti-stress Foods

01 ~ Celery
02 ~ Sunflower and sesame seeds,
raw shelled hemp seeds
03 ~ Brown rice
04 ~ Cabbage
05 ~ Almonds
06 ~ Berries
07 ~ Cucumbers
08 ~ Bananas
09 ~ Garlic
10 ~ Lettuce

And Five to Avoid

1 x Caffeine
2 x Alcohol
3 x Sugar and sugary foods
4 x Salt and salty foods
5 x Foods high in saturated fat

Ten Stress-relieving Supplements

01 ~ Vitamin B complex
02 ~ Magnesium
03 ~ Siberian ginseng
04 ~ Liquorice root
05 ~ Astragalus
06 ~ Valerian
07 ~ Rhodiola
08 ~ A good-quality antioxidant formula
09 ~ Blue-green algae
10 ~ Camomile, ginseng, lemon balm,
linden flower and nettle teas

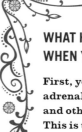

WHAT HAPPENS TO YOUR BODY WHEN YOU'RE STRESSED?

First, your brain prompts your adrenal gland to release adrenalin and other stress-related hormones. This is the fight or flight response – designed to deal with danger. It causes your heart rate to increase, you'll breathe faster and sweat more. Your muscles, heart, lungs and brain are given priority fuel and all your other body systems are subdued.

Why does all this happen? Because your body is gearing you up to take immediate action – fight or flight. When the danger or perceived danger is over, hormone levels and body systems return to normal. No harm done.

Problems arise only when the source of stress is prolonged. So an ongoing heavy workload, financial worries, troublesome relatives, conflict with your partner – all of these situations could cause your body to be in stress mode, a heightened state of alert, for far too long.

Abnormally raised levels of stress hormones can upset blood-sugar levels and raise blood pressure. You may feel tired, anxious, irritable and tearful. Stress can even lead to weight gain. That's because it depletes your body of vital nutrients, messes with your digestion and slows metabolism.

THE LIBIDO PLAN

Are you remembering to have sex? Sounds like a silly question. After all, you're engaged to be married, you can't get enough of one another – isn't that right? You'd be surprised how many brides (and grooms) I've met who forget all this, though, because they're so wrapped up in choosing favours and buttonholes and all those other wedding details. They're so focused on the day itself, they've lost track of the reasons it's happening. And when your mind is concentrating on other matters, sex is often neglected. An important point: there is no right or wrong amount of sex to have. I'm not about to prescribe you a sex diet – Monday, missionary position for twenty minutes, Tuesday . . . Imagine that! What does concern me is when sex becomes less frequent, or less satisfying, at a time when you should be closer than ever. There are some medications and medical conditions that can affect libido, so it's worth asking your doctor to investigate if you or your partner believes it could be an issue. And if you're experiencing any sort of tension in your relationship, this will affect how you feel about sex and how easily you become aroused. I'm not a relationship counsellor, so I can't advise you on this or suggest a diet to switch off your emotions. All I'll say is that sexual issues have a way of becoming more complex if you don't talk about them. You probably know what I'm going to say next. A very likely reason you're not feeling sexy is you're not eating the right foods. And this I most definitely can help you with. Wedding-planning stress, lack of sleep, big-day nerves – they're all factors which affect your sex life. Ironically, good sex is one of the best stress relievers there is, so you need to start eating well. Even if you don't think you're stressed, if your diet and lifestyle are unhealthy you're unlikely to look or feel your sexiest. Nutritional deficiencies can have a detrimental effect on your hormones, glands and organs, playing havoc with your sex drive. So let's get it sorted. Statistics show that most couples don't get down to it on their wedding night because they're too tired (or tipsy!), but there's no excuse on honeymoon.

Eat Yourself Sexy

If you've read Part One and you're following my plan, then you will have a healthy, balanced diet. If you know you're not quite giving it 100 per cent, or you'd just like some extra insurance, start taking a daily multivitamin and mineral complex supplement, to correct any nutritional imbalances.

A regular intake of good-quality protein is important – the best sources are sprouted seeds, soya beans (sometimes called edamames, pronounced *ed a mammies*), quinoa, tofu, fish, and lean chicken. Don't scrimp on whole-grains, fresh fruit and veg either.

The mineral zinc is essential for the production of sex hormones, sperm and female lubrication. The B group of vitamins are needed for sex hormones too – plus they support your adrenal glands, helping you deal with stress, reduce lethargy and boost mood. Find zinc in nuts and seeds, beans, eggs, wholegrains and lean meat. And get your fill of B vits from wholegrains, green leafy veg, beans, tuna, chicken, figs, poppy seeds, raw shelled hemp seeds, dates, and nuts such as brazil nuts.

Essential fatty acids (EFAs) are needed for sex hormone production.

Eat plenty of oily fish and flaxseed oil, gold of pleasure seed oil and consider an evening primrose or starflower oil supplement.

The following foods are my favourite sources of the nutrients I've just talked about, and good foods to choose if you want added sparks between the sheets.

Gillian's Top Ten Libido-boosting Foods

1. **Sauerkraut** – rich in compounds that strengthen the liver, where sex hormones are formed
2. **Raspberries/strawberries** – rich in vitamin C, for circulation, and the seeds contain zinc
3. **Pumpkin seeds** – packed with EFAs and zinc
4. **Quinoa** – top source of protein, B vits and zinc. It is nutritionally nourishing to your kidneys, and you need these little devils in fine fettle to keep up your sexual strength!
5. **Garlic** – increases blood flow to your sex organs
6. **Oats** – contain the zinc, protein, vitamin E and selenium needed for a healthy reproductive system, particularly sperm. There's a good reason for the phrase 'sow your wild oats'.
7. **Raw shelled hemp seeds** – crammed with EFAs (plus zinc)
8. **Ginger** – increases blood flow to your sex organs
9. **Cinnamon** – boosts blood flow to genitals and helps balance blood sugar for stamina
10. **Asparagus** – loaded with B vitamins including folic acid

And Five Sex-drive Saboteurs

1. **Alcohol** – loosens inhibitions, but also gives him brewer's droop. Booze severely depletes your levels of B vits too.
2. **Caffeine** – just one to one and a half cups a day of coffee, regular black tea, sodas or colas can diminish your sex life, because of the high content of caffeine in these drinks. Caffeine impedes the brain chemical adenosine, which keeps the happy chemical dopamine in proper balance. Instead, drink a rotation of herbal teas such as nettle, dandelion and red clover, or simply hot water with lemon.
3. **Sugar** – regular white sugar causes imbalances in your brain, as cell membranes thicken and swell. Sugar saps your body of brain-building vitamins and minerals; it also interferes with your levels of glucose, the brain's fuel, causing an increase in disruptive free radicals, which further destroy brain cells and neurons. But your brain is your turn-on mechanism for good sex. As a result, too much sugar kills sex life. I'm not saying that you can't ever eat a sweet. Just don't overdo it, and be aware of the effects of getting 'sugared out' – not that great sex and gaining weight.

4. Chocolate – most of us think of chocolate as a mood-boosting aphrodisiac food but I'm telling you that it has the opposite effect. Why? Because the chocolate most of us reach for is loaded with sugar, saturated fat, additives and calories. Not only will it trigger blood-sugar imbalances – and a short burst of energy followed by fatigue – but studies show it can also trigger feelings of guilt and depression. And nothing can dampen your libido more than a combination of fatigue, guilt and depression! Chocolate cravings might be a sign of low levels of minerals such as magnesium and chromium, or blood-sugar imbalances, which need to be checked out. If you crave chocolate, opt for cacao bits or powder instead (find them in the health-food store). Eat the cacao with a naturally sweet food such as fruit. Heaven! Cacao, the actual cocoa bean, is one of the highest natural sources of magnesium. That's why you sometimes crave chocolate: it's the body's way of telling you that it really needs magnesium. However, chocolate is not the solution, whereas cacao bits are a fine way to boost your body's supply of this particular mineral. A diet high in magnesium protects against the symptoms of hypertension, diabetes, heart disease, joint problems and pre-menstrual tension.

5. Trans Fats – or bad fats from poor-quality oils, fried foods, junk and processed foods, potato chips, crisps, baked goods and fatty meats, negatively affect the brain and sex life by blocking the conversion of good fats into essential brain fats. Unfavourable trans-fat blockers prevent the formation of healthy fats. This creates sexual lethargy.

Sexy Supplements

❤ Horny goat weed and ginkgo biloba – both these herbs improve circulation to your genitals, increasing arousal. Horny goat weed may also increase testosterone.

❤ Damiana – has a direct stimulant effect on the genitals, increasing sensitivity and producing tingling

❤ Miura puama – ginkgo biloba, positively affects your brain chemicals, so you're more in the mood for sex

❤ Siberian ginseng – this is an adaptogen, meaning it helps your body adapt to stress. A good choice for busy brides and grooms (for more on stress, see page 104).

❤ Agnus castus (also called Chaste Berry) – may boost libido in women if a hormone imbalance is to blame

❤ **Aveena sativa** – made from oats, has been found to increase sexual appetite. You can get this in liquid tincture from the health-food store.

❤ **Wild yam** – can help hormonal balance. Best when taken after ovulation, in the second half of your cycle.

❤ **Red clover** – a favourite with women hoping to boost their fertility, this blood-cleansing herb (available in tincture form) is renowned for its high vitamin content

Gillian says . . .

A word of caution: there's no point trying all these herbs at once. Apart from breaking the bank, if one of them works, how will you know which one it is? Pick the one which seems to fit your symptoms best and give it a go for a couple of months – it may take time for the effects to kick in.

TRY A LITTLE TANTRA TONIGHT . . .

Tantric sex is nothing to be scared of. It's not about doing it for hours on end or in strange positions (although who am I to stop you?). In fact, it's an ancient art designed to help you awaken and share your sexual energy.

Pelvic bouncing is a simple but surprisingly effective tantric exercise you can try together tonight.

❤ Lie on your back, feet flat on the floor or bed, knees raised. With your arms by your sides, palms up, breathe deeply for a few minutes, letting all your tension go.
❤ Now, press your heels into the floor and raise your hips.
❤ Bounce your pelvis up and down, rhythmically – you can play some lively music if it helps. Go at whatever speed you like.
❤ It's hard at first and you may feel like giving up, but hang on in there. Soon the momentum will build and it'll become almost effortless.

Pelvic bouncing charges your whole body with energy and makes you feel joyous and alive (not to mention ready for anything . . .).

Love on the Menu

On waking, drink a cup of hot water and lemon.

Breakfast
Exotic fruit salad with passion fruit, pomegranate, mango and goji berries

Mid-morning snack
Veggie juice of celery, beetroot, cucumber, carrots and a small piece of ginger

Lunch
Baked vegetables and quinoa (page 166)

Mid-afternoon snack
Handful of pumpkin seeds and a couple of Brazil nuts

Dinner
Steamed sea bass with lemon and asparagus (page 162)

Evening snack
A couple of figs

Special sexy treat
Dates rolled in carob powder or cacao bits (find them in health-food shops)

Dear Gillian,
It's OK to blow it all on honeymoon, right? My fiancé
has booked us into a five-star, all-inclusive Caribbean
resort and I don't want to waste his money!
Shelley, 35, Nottingham

Lucky you! And what are you asking me for, anyway? I signed up to
work with you until your wedding day. And you promised to stick to my
programme until you said, 'I do'. So, is it OK to 'blow it all on honeymoon'?
Well, that's entirely up to you, Shelley!

What you'll probably find, though, and experience has made me
pretty certain of this, is that you won't *want* to.

By the time your honeymoon arrives, you'll have achieved all the goals
you set, back on page 12. You'll be feeling fantastic,
full of vitality and confidence. You'll be showered in compliments from the
moment you wake on your wedding day. I don't believe your natural response
to all this will be to think, 'Mmm, fried chicken from the cheap takeaway.'

On the contrary, most people who follow my programme find it becomes
a way of life. Their taste buds seem to change so the foods they're drawn
towards are the fresh, healthy, delicious options. They've re-educated
their body and mind to reject the processed, fatty, sugary junk they once
survived on.

The danger with all-inclusive holidays is people thinking that because
it's there, they *have* to eat or drink it. And you might think, 'It's only two
weeks,' but it's amazing the effect constant grazing, creamy cocktails
round the pool and banquets every evening for fourteen days can have!

So my advice, as you've asked for it, is to carry on as you are. Listen to
your body and eat what it's asking you for. Consider whether or not you're
actually hungry before you head to the buffet a second time.

All-inclusive isn't all bad, though. The plus is that there's usually a huge
variety of food and drink on offer. And remember that variety is a healthy
eater's best friend. So you'll be able to keep up your diet of abundance,
without having to do the shopping or cooking yourself! I imagine you'll find
a whole rainbow of exotic fruit and veg in the Caribbean, exciting new
spices, fish so fresh it hops straight from the sea onto your plate. So enjoy –
prop up the juice bar all day. And then, if you still fancy that sundowner
cocktail, go for it. It is your honeymoon, after all!

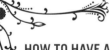

HOW TO HAVE A SEXIER HONEYMOON

You and your husband have soaked up your time in the limelight and now it's just the two of you. If you've been following my programme for some time, you'll expect to feel energized and sexy on honeymoon.

Don't be surprised, though, if you spend the first few days sleeping more than usual – napping on your sun lounger or sneaking off for siestas. You put hours of effort into organizing your wedding; it was a busy, sometimes stressful time. Many newly-weds have confessed to me that once their big day was over, and the adrenalin wore off, they simply felt shattered.

So, again, my advice would be to listen to your body and have all the naps you want for the first few days. Just remember that overeating and drinking lots of alcohol will zap your energy stores even more.

Instead, you and your new husband can fill up on antioxidant-packed fresh fruit, raw salads, exotic pomegranates, passion fruit, zinc-rich fish – and energize yourselves with romantic walks and swims. Check out my list of libido-boosting foods on page 111.

Don't forget to take advantage of all the romantic services usually on offer to honeymooners in all-inclusive resorts too. Think private, candlelit dinners on the beach and indulgent spa sessions for two. You'll soon get into the honeymoon groove and see your sex drive soar!

RECIPES

BREAKFASTS

Porridge oats with vanilla

SERVES 2 | PREP TIME 1 MINUTE
COOKING TIME 5 MINUTES
150g oats
600ml water
half a vanilla pod or a few drops of vanilla essence
1 tbsp sunflower seeds

Place the oats, water and vanilla in a small pan, bring to the boil and simmer for 5 minutes. Transfer to a small bowl, scatter over the seeds and serve.

Oats and rice milk

Oats are delicious raw. Simply serve with rice milk. You might think it a little harsh to start with, but do give it a go.

SERVES 1 | PREP TIME 1 MINUTE
75g oats
120–150ml rice milk
2 tsp agave syrup (optional)

Place the oats in a bowl and add the milk. Stir well, leave to stand for a few minutes, then drizzle with agave syrup, if desired.

Granola-style breakfast cereal

This is a great breakfast. You can eat it dry or pour either rice milk or natural yoghurt over it. It keeps well in an airtight tin for 3–4 days.

SERVES 2 | PREP TIME 2 MINUTES
COOKING TIME 12 MINUTES
30g porridge oats
30g barley flakes
2 tsp agave syrup
half a teaspoon vanilla essence
3 tbsp hemp seeds
3 tbsp sunflower seeds

1. Preheat the oven to 200C/gas mark 6.
2. Mix all the ingredients together in a bowl and scatter over a baking tray.
3. Bake for 12 minutes, then allow to cool and store in an airtight container.

Barley flake porridge

Agave syrup is a natural sweetener that is made from the sap of cactus plants. It is available in most health food shops and makes a great alternative to honey and other sweeteners.

SERVES 2 | PREP TIME 2 MINUTES
COOKING TIME 10 MINUTES
150g barley flakes
600ml cold water
2 tsp agave syrup (optional)
sprinkle of freshly grated nutmeg (optional)

Place the barley flakes and water in a small saucepan, bring to the boil and simmer for 10 minutes. Serve with agave syrup and nutmeg, if desired.

Fruit salad

SERVES 2 | PREP TIME 5 MINUTES
1 kiwi, peeled and sliced
2 peaches, sliced
1 punnet blueberries
1 punnet raspberries
1 orange, cut into segments
juice of a second orange

Mix all the ingredients together and serve. It will keep well in the fridge for 24 hours.

Goji berry dried fruit salad

SERVES 2 | PREP TIME 5 MINUTES
125g goji berries
125g prunes
125g dried apricots (unsulphured)
125g dried figs
half a teaspoon of cinnamon powder

Put all the ingredients in a bowl and just cover with water.
Leave to soak for a few hours or overnight.

Exotic passion in a fruit salad

SERVES 2 | PREP TIME 5 MINUTES
2 passion fruit (pulp)
1 papaya, deseeded and chopped
1 pomegranate
1 mango, stoned and chopped
2 kiwi, peeled and sliced
1 peach, stoned and sliced

Mix all the ingredients together and serve chilled. Save leftovers,
if there are any, for a snack later in the day.

Warm it up fruity salad

SERVES 2 | PREP TIME 5 MINUTES
COOKING TIME 15–20 MINUTES
2 apples, cored and sliced
2 pears, cored and sliced
juice of 1 orange
sprinkle of cinnamon

1. Preheat the oven to 180C/gas mark 4.
2. Arrange the fruit in a shallow ovenproof dish, pour the orange juice over it and sprinkle with cinnamon.
3. Bake in the oven for 15–20 minutes, until soft.

Baked butter beans on toast

Sprouted hemp bread is now available in many health food shops. You could also try spelt, quinoa or rye bread. Make sure your choice of bread is free from additives and preservatives.

SERVES 2 | PREP TIME 2 MINUTES
COOKING TIME 20 MINUTES
400g can butter beans
400g can tomatoes
4 slices hemp bread, lightly toasted

1. Place the beans and tomatoes in a small pan and simmer gently for 20 minutes.
2. Spoon it over the hemp toast and serve immediately.

For more traditional beans on toast, use haricot beans. In health food shops you can also buy really healthy baked beans that are free from sugar and artificial sweeteners.

Scrambled egg with grilled tomatoes

A really good non-stick pan will allow you to cook food with no oil whatsoever. If you don't have a non-stick pan then use a teaspoon of sunflower or hemp oil mixed with 1 tablespoon of water.

SERVES 2 | PREP TIME 2 MINUTES
COOKING TIME 3 MINUTES
2 free-range organic eggs
2 tbsp cold water
1 pinch sea salt (optional)
4 vine-ripened tomatoes, cut in half

1. Preheat the grill or oven to 200C/gas mark 6.
2. Whisk the eggs and water together in a small bowl, but don't add the salt yet.
3. Place the tomatoes under the grill or in the oven.
4. Heat the non-stick pan: you can feel when it is warm by holding your hand 10 cm above it. Then add the salt to the eggs, whisk once and quickly pour into the pan. Start stirring immediately with a wooden spoon or spatula.
5. Continue to stir, ensuring that you don't allow the eggs on the edge of the pan to cook more quickly than those in the centre. They should look soft and light. Remove the eggs from the heat while they still appear slightly wet, as they will continue to cook in the pan.
6. Remove the tomatoes from the grill or oven once they are cooked but not yet brown.
7. Transfer to 2 warm plates. Spoon the eggs next to the tomatoes and serve.

Herbal omelette

SERVES 2 | PREP TIME 2 MINUTES
COOKING TIME 3 MINUTES
4 free-range organic eggs
2 tbsp water
2 tbsp chopped fresh parsley or chervil
1 tbsp olive oil
5 cherry tomatoes, cut in half

1. Whisk the eggs and water together in a small bowl, then
add the herbs and whisk again.
2. Heat the oil in a non-stick omelette pan and pour in the eggs.
Leave for 30 seconds for the base to set and then, using a spatula
or wooden spoon, draw the egg mix from the outside of the pan
into the centre. Repeat all the way around the pan until the
omelette looks ruffled and fluffy.
3. Leave the omelette for 30 seconds to set then loosen the
edges of the omelette and transfer to a serving plate. Divide
the omelette in half and serve with the cherry tomatoes.

Baked mushrooms with tomato

SERVES 2 | PREP TIME 4–5 MINUTES
COOKING TIME 20–30 MINUTES
2 large flat mushrooms (125g)
half a teaspoon of olive oil or gold of pleasure seed oil
1 tsp wheat-free tamari sauce
1 large beef tomato, sliced
1 pinch sea salt
1 tbsp chopped fresh parsley

1. Preheat the oven to 180C/gas mark 4.
2. Remove the stalks from the mushrooms and place them on a baking tray.
3. Divide the oil and tamari sauce between the mushroom's centres and arrange the tomato slices on the mushroom's cups.
4. Transfer to the preheated oven and bake for 20–30 minutes. Transfer to 2 warm serving plates and sprinkle with a little salt and parsley.

Gold of pleasure seed oil is a new variety of oil extracted from the seed of a plant found growing in flax crops as a weed. It is very high in the Omegas, so worth seeking out. If you can't find it, then olive oil is an excellent alternative.

SMOOTHIES

Mad for mango

Smoothies can be made in a blender or juicer. If you are using a juicer, some of the fibre from the fruit will be removed and you will get a slightly thinner texture. If you are using a blender, you sometimes need to add a little water.

SERVES 1 | PREP TIME 2 MINUTES
1 mango, peeled, stoned and roughly chopped
1 pear, peeled and cored
1 banana, roughly chopped

Place all the ingredients in a blender or juicer and blend until smooth.

Sunny strawberry

If you are on a weight-loss plan, I advocate no dairy products at all and would suggest you omit the yoghurt. However, if you are simply looking for vitality and good health for the big day then a little natural yoghurt, free from additives or preservatives, will do no harm.

SERVES 1 | PREP TIME 2 MINUTES
1 punnet strawberries
1 banana, peeled and roughly chopped
125ml pot natural yoghurt (no additives or sweeteners)

Place all the ingredients in a blender and blend until smooth.

Passionate Pear

SERVES 1 | PREP TIME 5 MINUTES
2 pears, peeled and cored
1 tsp lemon juice
1 passion fruit (pulp)
1 handful flaxseeds

Place all the ingredients in a blender or juicer, except the seeds, and blend until smooth. Pour into a glass and scatter over the flaxseeds.

Nectarine berry boost

SERVES 2 | PREP TIME 2 MINUTES
2 ripe nectarines, stoned
1 punnet raspberries
1 punnet strawberries, hulled
1 handful shelled hemp seeds

Place all the ingredients in a blender or juicer, except the seeds, and blend until smooth. Pour into a glass and scatter over the hemp seeds.

Pink grapefuit juice

SERVES 1 | PREP TIME 2 MINUTES
2 pink grapefruit, peeled

Pass the flesh of the grapefruit through a juicer and
serve chilled.

Pineapple and papaya

SERVES 1 | PREP TIME 5 MINUTES
1 small pineapple, peeled and cored
1 papaya, deseeded and peeled

Place all the ingredients in a blender or juicer and blend
until smooth.

SOUPS

Aduki bean and corn broth with avocado

Aduki beans, the ultimate weight-loss bean, are now available in cans in health food stores and large supermarkets.

SERVES 2 | PREP TIME 5 MINUTES
COOKING TIME 10 MINUTES
400g can aduki beans
198g can organic corn
2 tsp vegetable bouillon powder
500ml boiling water
4 spring onions, chopped
1 celery stalk, sliced
2 tomatoes, deseeded and chopped
1 avocado, peeled, stoned and roughly crushed
2 handfuls fresh coriander
2 tbsp lemon juice

1. Drain the beans, and rinse then drain the corn. Leave to one side.
2. Place the water and stock in a medium-sized pan, then add the spring onions and celery. Bring it to the boil, add the beans, corn and tomatoes, and simmer for 10 minutes.
3. Mix the avocado with half the coriander and the lemon juice. Add the remaining coriander to the soup, and serve with the crushed avocado.

Creamy bean bisque

SERVES 2 | PREP TIME 10 MINUTES
COOKING TIME 20 MINUTES
420g can organic butter beans
1 onion, finely chopped
1 leek, finely chopped
2 garlic cloves
4 tbsp water
500ml boiling water
2 tsp organic bouillon powder
1 bay leaf
2 tbsp chopped fresh parsley, plus leaves to garnish
2 spring onions

1. Drain the beans and rinse well.
2. Place the onion, leek and garlic in a saucepan with 4 tablespoons of water and cook over a low heat for 3–4 minutes.
3. Add the boiling water and stock, bay leaf and parsley. Bring to the boil and simmer for 10 minutes.
4. Add the beans and simmer for a further 10 minutes.
5. Remove from the heat, discard the bay leaf and allow the soup to cool.
6. Blend the soup in a food processor or blender until smooth. Add the spring onions, garnish with some parsley leaves and serve.

Minestrone soup

SERVES 2 | PREP TIME 5 MINUTES
COOKING TIME 20 MINUTES
1 tbsp olive oil
1 tbsp water
1 medium onion, finely chopped
1 celery stalk, sliced
1 small carrot, peeled and sliced
2 garlic cloves, sliced
1 ltr boiling water
2 tsp wheat-free vegetable bouillon powder or
   2 vegetable stock cubes
1 small sweet potato, peeled and cut into 1 cm cubes
1 tbsp tomato puree
1 tsp dried mixed herbs
100g fine green beans, trimmed and cut into thirds
1 small leek, white part only, sliced
1 courgette, sliced
50g frozen peas
1 handful of fresh basil leaves to garnish

1. Place the oil, water, onion, celery and carrot in a medium-sized pan and cook over a moderate heat for 4–5 minutes until soft but not coloured.

2. Add the garlic, stir and cook for 1 minute, then add the boiling water and stock, sweet potato, tomato puree and mixed herbs. Cover and leave to simmer for 10 minutes, or until the potato is soft when pierced with a knife.

3. Add the green beans, leek and courgette and cook for 5 minutes. Add the peas and cook for a further 2 minutes. Remove from the heat, serve in large soup bowls and scatter with fresh basil leaves.

Soya bean soup

The secret to creating meals in minutes is having a tidy and organized kitchen with everything at hand. Frozen soya beans are now available in large supermarkets and in health food shops as well.

SERVES 2 | PREP TIME 5 MINUTES
COOKING TIME 6 MINUTES
2 sachets of miso soup or 2 stock cubes
500ml boiling water
4 spring onions (40g), finely sliced
2 celery stalks, finely sliced
250g frozen soya beans
1 handful fresh mint leaves

1. Place the miso soup or stock cubes in a medium-sized saucepan and pour over the boiling water.
2. Place over a high heat and bring to the boil. Add the onion and celery, but reserve the green top of the onion and a handful of celery to garnish.
3. Measure out the beans and add them to the pan, return the mixture to the boil and then add the mint. Cover the pan with a lid and leave to simmer for 4 minutes.
4. Remove from the heat, and blend until smooth.
5. Spoon into 2 bowls, top with the spring onion and celery, and serve.

Note that if you are using a glass blender you need to allow the mixture to cool slightly before blending, as it will be very hot.

Sweet corn and seaweed soup

This is a great, quick and satisfying soup. Ginger miso paste is available in the chilled section of most health food shops. Alternatively substitute with 1 sachet of dried miso soup mix.

SERVES 2 | PREP TIME 5–10 MINUTES
COOKING TIME 5 MINUTES
600ml water
3 tsp ginger miso paste
5cm piece fresh ginger, peeled and chopped
4 tbsp chopped fresh coriander
120g can organic sweet corn
2 tbsp arame seaweed

1. Place the water in a small pan with the ginger miso paste, ginger and coriander. Bring to the boil and add the sweet corn.
2. Simmer for 1–2 minutes then remove from the heat. Transfer to a warm soup bowl, sprinkle over the arame and serve.

Minted pea soup

This fantastic soup takes less than 10 minutes from start to finish, and it tastes amazing as well.

SERVES 2 | PREP TIME 2 MINUTES
COOKING TIME 6 MINUTES
1 large onion, finely chopped
1 tsp gold of pleasure seed oil or olive oil
1 tbsp water
500ml boiling water
1 tsp wheat-free vegetable bouillon powder or stock cube
200g frozen peas
1 large handful fresh mint leaves
nori sprinkles and a few fresh peas to garnish

1. Place the onion in a medium-sized saucepan with the oil and water. Cook over a moderate heat for 4 minutes, or until translucent and soft.
2. Add the boiling water and stock and peas, and simmer for 2 minutes.
3. Add the mint, remove from the heat and blend until smooth. Pour into 2 soup bowls and garnish with nori sprinkles and peas.

Thai-style roasted carrot soup

Kaffir lime leaves add a wonderful aromatic quality to this unusual soup. They are available frozen in oriental supermarkets and dried in most large supermarkets. Mostly associated with Thai cookery, lemon grass is a tough stalk that adds flavour and is usually removed from the food before it is eaten. Alternatively, you could use a little lemon peel.

**SERVES 2 | PREP TIME 10 MINUTES
COOKING TIME 50 MINUTES
450g peeled organic carrots cut in 6–7-cm lengths
1 stalk lemon grass
5cm piece fresh ginger, sliced
1 tsp coriander seeds
750ml boiling water
1 vegetable stock cube
2 kaffir lime leaves
4 tbsp chopped fresh coriander
2 spring onions, chopped**

1. Preheat the oven to 180C/gas mark 4.
2. Take a large piece of foil and place the carrots, lemon grass, ginger and coriander seeds in the centre. Scrunch the foil up around the carrots to create a 'tent'.
3. Transfer to the oven and bake for 25–30 minutes. The carrots should be tender when pierced with a knife.
4. Remove from the oven and allow them to cool in the foil. Remove the carrots and discard the seasonings. Take 1 piece of carrot, slice into half-cm pieces and keep to one side.
5. Place the boiling water, stock and kaffir lime leaves in a medium-sized saucepan, bring to the boil and simmer for 10 minutes. Add the carrots and simmer for a further 5 minutes.
6. Remove from the heat and allow to cool slightly, then remove the kaffir lime leaves and discard.
7. Transfer to a blender or food processor and blend until smooth.
8. Warm the soup through gently and pour into warm serving bowls. Scatter over the reserved carrot pieces, the fresh coriander and the spring onions and serve.

Watercress soup

Great as a starter or light lunch followed by a large salad.

SERVES 2 | PREP TIME 8–10 MINUTES
COOKING TIME 18–20 MINUTES
1 tbsp olive oil or gold of pleasure seed oil
2 tbsp water
1 medium onion, peeled and finely chopped
2 celery stalks, trimmed and sliced
1 medium sweet potato (around 150g), peeled and
  cut into roughly 2cm cubes
2 garlic cloves, peeled and crushed
500ml cold water
2 tsp organic vegetable bouillon powder
1 bag (100g) fresh watercress
1 tbsp pumpkin seeds (optional)

1. Heat the oil and 2 tablespoons water in a medium-sized saucepan and cook the onion and celery very gently for 1 minute. Add a little water and cook for 2 minutes, until it begins to soften. Stir in the sweet potato and garlic and cook for about another minute.

2. Pour over the rest of the water, stir in the bouillon powder and bring to the boil. Reduce the heat slightly and simmer for 15 minutes, until the potatoes are soft.

3. Remove from the heat and stir in the watercress. Stand for 2 minutes.

4. Blend until smooth with a hand blender, or cool for 10 minutes and then transfer to a liquidizer or food processor.

5. Warm it through gently, then ladle into deep bowls and serve. Sprinkle with pumpkin seeds, if desired.

Mushroom soup with julienne vegetables

Shiitake mushrooms are my favourite and are available in large supermarkets. As an alternative, you could use either chestnut or button mushrooms.

SERVES 2 | PREP TIME 5 MINUTES
COOKING TIME 20–25 MINUTES
750ml water
2 miso or vegetable stock cubes
1 leek, halved and sliced
1 celery stalk, sliced
1 onion, finely chopped
4 tbsp chopped fresh parsley
1 bay leaf
1 sprig of thyme
2 garlic cloves
200g shiitake mushrooms, plus a few to garnish
a few drops of truffle oil (optional)
Raw julienne vegetables:
1 carrot, peeled and cut into fine sticks (julienne)
1 celery stalk, very finely sliced
1 bok choy, finely shredded
1 handful chopped fresh parsley

1. Bring the water and stock cubes to the boil in a medium-sized pan. Add the leek, celery, onion, 2 tablespoons of parsley, the bay leaf, thyme and garlic.
2. Bring back to the boil, cover with a lid and then simmer for 20 minutes.
3. Add the mushrooms and simmer for 2–3 minutes.
4. Spoon the soup into warm serving bowls. Scatter some raw mushrooms and parsley over it.
5. Add the raw vegetables, sprinkle a few drops of truffle oil, if desired, and serve.

Cabbage and sage soup

There's a good amount of soup here, because I want you to freeze some of it so you have it to hand when you need it.

SERVES 2, PLUS EXTRA FOR FREEZING
PREP TIME 10 MINUTES | COOKING TIME 20–30 MINUTES
2 red onions, chopped
3 garlic cloves, peeled and crushed
4 carrots, peeled and chopped
1 head broccoli, florets only
1 white cabbage, shredded
6 new potatoes
1 ltr boiling water
3 tsp miso powder
1 large handful fresh sage
1 large handful fresh parsley, plus extra to garnish

1. Place all the ingredients, except the sage and parsley, in a large pan. Bring to the boil, cover and simmer for 20–30 minutes.
2. Throw in the parsley and sage at the end, but do not allow the herbs to cook.
3. Remove from the heat and blend until smooth.
4. Serve in 2 large warm bowls and sprinkle with a little parsley.

MAIN MEALS

Italian-style chicken with peppers, tomatoes and olives

SERVES 2 | PREP TIME 10 MINUTES
COOKING TIME 10–15 MINUTES
1 onion, finely chopped
1 tbsp olive oil
1 tbsp water
1 garlic clove, sliced
400g can organic chopped tomatoes
1 tsp balsamic vinegar
1 tsp dried marjoram
1 red pepper, cut into strips
200ml boiling water
1 tsp organic wheat-free bouillon powder
2 chicken breasts (150g each)
1 handful fresh basil, roughly torn
1 tbsp pitted black olives

1. Place the onion, oil and water in a medium-sized saucepan, using one that has a lid, and cook over a moderate heat for 4–5 minutes, until the onions are soft and translucent.
2. Add the garlic and cook for 1 minute, then add the tomatoes, vinegar, marjoram, pepper, boiling water and stock.
3. Bring to the boil and add the chicken breasts. Cover and simmer for 10–15 minutes, until the chicken is firm to the touch
4. Add the basil and olives. Serve with couscous or quinoa and a green salad.

Easy chicken stir-fry

SERVES 2 | PREP TIME 5 MINUTES
COOKING TIME 10 MINUTES
1 tbsp sesame oil
1 tbsp water
2 small chicken breasts (100g each), thinly sliced
1 red pepper, finely sliced
1 garlic clove, peeled and crushed
1 tsp Chinese five-spice powder
100g baby corn, halved lengthways
juice of 1 orange
1 tbsp wheat-free tamari sauce
1 tsp cornflour
100g mangetout
1 bok choy, cored and shredded
2 spring onions, chopped
1 handful fresh bean sprouts
1 tbsp cashew nuts, chopped
2 tbsp chopped fresh coriander

1. Heat the oil and water in a wok or a non-stick frying pan, add the chicken and cook for 2–3 minutes. Add the pepper, garlic, Chinese five-spice powder and corn then cook for another 3–4 minutes.

2. Place the orange juice, tamari sauce and cornflour in a small bowl and stir well. Set this to one side.

3. Add the mangetout and bok choy to the pan and cook for 2 minutes, then add the spring onions and cook for a further 30 seconds. Add the orange, tamari sauce and cornflour mixture and cook for another minute, until the sauce thickens.

4. Top with the bean sprouts, nuts and coriander and serve.

Light chicken and vegetable curry

SERVES 2 | PREP TIME 10 MINUTES
COOKING TIME 18–20 MINUTES
1 tbsp olive or sunflower oil
1 medium onion, peeled and sliced
150g boneless, skinless chicken breast (preferably free range
    or organic), cut into roughly 3-cm pieces
2 garlic cloves, peeled and crushed
half a teaspoon ground cumin
half a teaspoon ground coriander
half a teaspoon ground turmeric
3–4 cardamom pods
1 red or orange pepper, deseeded and cut into roughly 3-cm pieces
150g cauliflower florets (from half a small cauliflower)
75g green beans, trimmed and halved
4 medium tomatoes, quartered
300ml boiling water
1 organic vegetable stock cube
50g fresh or frozen peas
2 good handfuls baby spinach leaves (approx. 50g)
1 handful chopped fresh coriander (optional)

1. Heat the oil in a large saucepan and gently cook the onion
and chicken for 2–3 minutes until the chicken is very lightly
coloured all over. While sautéing add a little water, then add
the garlic and spices and cook together for about a minute
to release the flavours.

2. Stir in the pepper, cauliflower, green beans and tomatoes. Pour
over the water and stock. Bring it to the boil, then reduce the heat
slightly and simmer gently for 10 minutes, stirring occasionally.

3. Add the peas and spinach leaves and continue to simmer for
a further 2–3 minutes, until the peas are just tender and the
spinach is wilted.

4. Serve in large bowls and garnish with plenty of fresh coriander,
if desired.

Nutty bean loaf

This can be reserved for a weekend or special occasion.
You will love it.

**SERVES 6 | PREP TIME 15–20 MINUTES
COOKING TIME 40 MINUTES**
1 tbsp olive oil
2 slender leeks, trimmed and thinly sliced
1 medium onion, peeled and chopped
2 garlic cloves, peeled and crushed
**2 medium carrots, peeled and coarsely grated
  (prepared weight approx. 125g)**
410g can cannellini beans in water, drained and rinsed
200g shelled mixed nuts, roughly chopped
1 tbsp organic vegetable bouillon powder
3 tbsp roughly chopped fresh flat leaf parsley

1. Preheat the oven to 190C/gas mark 5. Lightly oil a 900g
loaf tin and line the base with baking parchment.
2. Heat the oil in a large saucepan and cook the leeks gently
for 4–5 minutes, until softened, stirring regularly. Set the
leeks aside.
3. Put the onion, garlic, carrots, cannellini beans, nuts and
bouillon in a food processor and blend for a few seconds. Remove
the lid, push the mixture down with a spatula, then blend for
a few more seconds until the mixture comes together but
retains some texture.
4. Transfer to a large mixing bowl. Stir in the leeks and parsley.
Spoon the mixture into the tin you have prepared and smooth the
surface. Bake the loaf in the centre of the oven for 35–40 minutes,
until golden brown, and set.
5. Remove the loaf from the oven and stand for 5 minutes before
loosening the edges with a round-bladed knife and turning it
out of the tin. Slice thickly and serve either warm or cold with
a lightly dressed fresh green salad.

This loaf is particularly good served with my tasty tomato and
pepper sauce (see page 203), but it also goes well with a rich onion
gravy. Wrap any leftovers in foil and keep chilled for up to 2 days.

Thirty-minute ratatouille

SERVES 3–4 | PREP TIME 10 MINUTES
COOKING TIME 20 MINUTES

2 tbsp olive oil or gold of pleasure seed oil
1 tbsp water
2 onions, peeled and chopped
2 garlic cloves, peeled and finely sliced
1 red pepper, deseeded and cut into roughly 3-cm pieces
1 yellow pepper, deseeded and cut into roughly 3-cm pieces
2 medium sweet potatoes, peeled and cut into roughly
    2-cm pieces
400g can chopped tomatoes
half a teaspoon dried mixed herbs
1 organic vegetable stock cube
2 medium courgettes, trimmed and sliced
410g can cannellini beans in water, drained and rinsed (optional)
basil leaves (optional)

1. Heat the oil and water in a large saucepan and cook the onion gently for 3 minutes, until softened but not coloured. Add the garlic, peppers and sweet potatoes and cook for 2 minutes.
2. Stir in the tomatoes, then refill the can with cold water and add to the pan. Sprinkle with the herbs and crumble over the stock cube. Stir well and bring to the boil, then reduce the heat slightly and simmer gently for 10 minutes. Stir occasionally.
3. Add the courgettes and beans and cook, stirring regularly, for 3–4 minutes, or until the beans are hot and the courgettes tender, adding a little extra water if the sauce seems too thick.
4. Top with torn basil leaves, if desired, and serve with a fresh, crunchy side salad.

This will keep well in the fridge for 1–2 days, but make sure you reheat it gently so the vegetables don't break up. Alternatively, serve 2 portions as a main meal and, adding a little extra water, whiz the rest into a flavoursome soup.

Puy lentil, leek and kale stew

SERVES 4–5 | PREP TIME 10 MINUTES
COOKING TIME 30 MINUTES

2 tbsp olive oil
1 tbsp water
1 medium onion, peeled and chopped
2 celery stalks, trimmed and sliced
2 carrots, peeled and sliced
2 garlic cloves, peeled and crushed
200g puy lentils, rinsed in a sieve and drained
1.25 ltr boiling water
1 organic vegetable stock cube
1 tsp organic vegetable bouillon powder
2 sweet potatoes, peeled and cut into roughly 3-cm pieces
2 slender leeks, trimmed and sliced
100g curly kale or savoy cabbage, roughly shredded
   with tough stalks removed

1. Heat the oil and water in a large saucepan and gently cook the onion, celery and carrots for 5 minutes, stirring occasionally, until they begin to soften but not to change colour. Add the garlic and lentils and cook with the vegetables for about 1 minute, stirring constantly.

2. Crumble the stock cube in the boiling water, sprinkle with the bouillon powder and add this stock to the vegetable mix. Bring to the boil, then reduce the heat slightly and simmer, uncovered, for 12 minutes, stirring occasionally.

3. Add the sweet potatoes and leeks and simmer for a further 8 minutes, stirring occasionally until the lentils are just tender (adding a little extra water if necessary). Finish by stirring in the kale and cooking for 1–2 minutes until softened. Ladle into warmed bowls and serve.

This one-pot meal is really filling and tastes amazing. It keeps very well for a couple of days in the fridge. Heat through until piping hot, adding a little extra water if the lentils have soaked up too much of the stock overnight. You can also add extra water and whiz any leftover stew into a delicious, hearty lentil soup.

Beany root vegetable stew

**SERVES 4 | PREP TIME 10–15 MINUTES
COOKING TIME 30 MINUTES**
2 tbsp olive oil or gold of pleasure seed oil
1 tbsp water
1 medium onion, peeled and chopped
8 shallots, peeled
2 celery stalks, trimmed and sliced
4 medium carrots, peeled and sliced
2 medium parsnips, peeled and cut into roughly 2cm pieces
half a celeriac, peeled and cut into roughly 2cm pieces
    (prepared weight approx. 300g)
2 garlic cloves, peeled and finely chopped
750ml boiling water
1 organic vegetable stock cube
1 tbsp tomato puree
1 small bay leaf
leaves from a small bunch fresh thyme leaves (about 1 tbsp)
    or 1 tsp dried mixed herbs
1 x 410g cans aduki beans in water, drained and rinsed
1 tbsp cornflour mixed with 2 tbsp cold water to form a paste
chopped fresh flat leaf parsley

1. Heat the oil and water in a large saucepan and gently cook
the onion, shallots, celery, carrots, parsnips and celeriac for 10–12
minutes, stirring regularly, until they begin to soften and colour
very lightly, but without burning. Add the garlic and cook for
about a minute.
2. Dissolve the stock cube in the water and pour over the
vegetables. Stir in the tomato puree, bay leaf and thyme or mixed
herbs. Bring to the boil, then reduce the heat, cover and simmer
gently for 15 minutes, stirring occasionally.
3. Add the beans and cook for 2–3 minutes until the beans are hot
and the vegetables are tender. Stir in the cornflour mixture and
cook for 1–2 minutes until the sauce thickens, stirring regularly.
Ladle on to warmed plates and sprinkle with lots of chopped
parsley. Serve with lightly cooked, shredded savoy cabbage or
green beans.

Vegetable korma

If you are a curry fan then this mild but tasty fat-free dish should really hit the spot. It can be made just as successfully with broccoli as an alternative to courgette.

SERVES 2 | PREP TIME 5 MINUTES
COOKING TIME 20 MINUTES
500ml water
1 large onion, finely chopped
2 garlic cloves, peeled and chopped
half a teaspoon coriander seeds
1 tsp ground coriander
1 tsp turmeric
1 tsp ginger powder
3 cardamom pods
200g turnips, peeled and chopped
350g courgettes, sliced
4 tbsp ground almonds
3 tbsp chopped fresh coriander

1. Place 100 ml of the water in a non-stick frying pan with the onion, garlic, coriander, turmeric, ginger and cardamom. Cook over a gentle heat until the onion has softened.
2. Stir in the turnips and courgettes, add another 300 ml of water, cover and simmer for 15 minutes, stirring occasionally and adding more water as required.
3. Add the almonds and cook for a further 2–3 minutes, so they are able to thicken the sauce.
4. Remove from the heat and scatter with fresh coriander. Serve with brown rice and red onion and cucumber raita (see below).

Red onion and cucumber raita

1 small red onion, finely chopped
quarter of a cucumber, finely cubed
2 tsp rice vinegar

Mix all the ingredients together in a small bowl and serve with curry.

Baked salmon parcels

SERVES 2 | PREP TIME 10 MINUTES
COOKING TIME 20–25 MINUTES
1 medium courgette, trimmed and thinly sliced
1 yellow pepper, deseeded and cut into thin strips
10 cherry tomatoes
2 fresh salmon fillets (150g each, preferably wild or organic)
4 slices of fresh lemon
1 tbsp olive or vegetable oil
1 spring onion, trimmed and finely sliced
1 stalk lemon grass, chopped
2cm piece fresh ginger, sliced

1. Preheat the oven to 200C/gas mark 6. Cut two large squares of foil and place on a baking sheet.
2. Divide the courgette, pepper and tomatoes between the foil sheets and top with the salmon fillets. Place two slices of lemon on each piece of fish, drizzle with the oil and sprinkle with the spring onion, lemon grass and ginger. Bring the foil up around the fish and vegetables to create two neat parcels. Pinch the edges to seal.
3. Bake for 20 minutes until the fish and vegetables are just cooked. Remove from the oven and allow to stand for 3 minutes. Open very carefully – the parcels will be hot. Lift the fish and vegetables on to two plates using a spatula. Pour the cooking juices over. Serve with a large mixed side salad.

You can make these parcels up to 12 hours in advance and keep them in the fridge until you're ready to cook them. Add 3–4 minutes to the cooking time if you're baking them straight from chilled.

Warm salmon salad

SERVES 2 | PREP TIME 6–8 MINUTES
COOKING TIME 12–15 MINUTES
2 tbsp olive oil
2 tsp good quality balsamic vinegar
2 spring onions, trimmed and finely chopped
2 salmon fillets (approx. 150g each), preferably wild or organic
75g green beans, trimmed
2 large handfuls spinach, watercress and rocket salad
8 cherry tomatoes, halved
50g small pitted black olives in olive oil, drained

1. Preheat the oven to 200C/gas mark 6. Mix the oil, vinegar and spring onions in a small, shallow ovenproof dish. Add the salmon fillets (they should fit fairly snugly) and turn them so they are coated in the dressing.

2. Place the dish in the centre of the oven and bake the salmon in the marinade for 12–15 minutes until just cooked.

3. While the salmon is baking, boil the green beans for 3 minutes, then drain in a sieve and rinse under running water until cold.

4. Arrange the salad, beans, tomatoes and olives on 2 plates. Remove the salmon from the oven and leave to stand for 2–3 minutes, then lift each fillet carefully, using a fish slice, on to the salad. Spoon a little warm marinade over each dish and serve.

Salmon and savoy cabbage 'lasagne'

This dish gets its name from the layers of cabbage and salmon that resemble a traditional lasagne. It is very attractive and full of flavour, and is a really good dish if you are entertaining.

SERVES 4 | PREP TIME 10 MINUTES
COOKING TIME 10 MINUTES
1 large savoy cabbage
2 tsp sesame oil
3 tbsp boiling water
zest of 1 lemon
2 tsp brown rice vinegar
1 tsp tamari sauce
1 salmon fillet (300g)
8 spring onions, finely chopped

1. Remove 5 outer leaves from the cabbage. Take a sharp knife and trim the base of these leaves, cutting away the tough central vein. This will leave a small 'v' shape in each leaf.
2. Bring a large pan of water to the boil, add the leaves and boil for 2 minutes. Drain and rinse in cold water.
3. Finely shred the remaining cabbage and place in a non-stick pan with the sesame oil and water. Set to a moderate heat and cook until the cabbage has just wilted, then add the lemon zest, rice vinegar and tamari sauce. Remove from the heat and leave in the pan to cool.
4. Place the salmon fillet on a chopping board and, using a sharp knife, slice the fish horizontally into half-cm slices.
5. Take a large piece of greaseproof paper and place a cabbage leaf in the centre. Cover with a third of the salmon slices. Place a third of the shredded cabbage mixture on top, using a slotted spoon. Cover with a second cabbage leaf and repeat the process until you have completed the lasagne. Drizzle a little of the juice left over from cooking the shredded cabbage over the top and wrap the paper firmly around the salmon and cabbage 'lasagne'.
6. Place in a bamboo steamer over a pan of boiling water and steam for 7–10 minutes, or until the parcel feels firm to the touch.
7. Remove from the steamer, unwrap and slice into 4 wedges. Transfer to 4 warm serving plates, drizzle over any remaining juices and scatter the chopped spring onions on top. Serve immediately.

Baked white fish with minted peas

SERVES 2 | PREP TIME 5 MINUTES
COOKING TIME 15 MINUTES
2 cod or haddock fillets, skinless (125g each)
juice of 1 lemon
2 tbsp chopped fresh parsley or chervil
2 tsp olive oil

1. Preheat the oven to 200C/gas mark 6.
2. Take 2 pieces of unbleached greaseproof paper, approx. 20cm by 20cm.
3. Place the fish on the paper, add the lemon juice, parsley and oil, then fold the paper up like a parcel.
4. Place the parcels on a baking sheet and cook in the preheated oven for 10–15 minutes, depending on how thick the pieces of fish are.
5. Remove from the oven and transfer the parcels to 2 serving plates. Serve with the crushed minty peas (see below), a large salad and brown rice.

Crushed minty peas

Mirin is a Japanese liquid sweetener that is fermented from rice and has quite a distinctive flavour. It is available in oriental shops and large supermarkets.

125g peas
1 handful fresh mint leaves
1 tsp mirin

Place the peas in boiling water for 30 seconds, add the mint and drain immediately. Place in a small bowl, crush with the back of a fork and add a teaspoon of mirin.

Baked Icelandic cod with garlic and parsley

SERVES 2 | PREP TIME 5 MINUTES
COOKING TIME 10 MINUTES
2 Icelandic cod or haddock fillets (150g each)
2 tbsp olive oil, plus extra for greasing
2 tbsp chopped fresh parsley
2 small garlic cloves, peeled and crushed
2 tbsp pine nuts

1. Preheat the oven to 200C/gas mark 6.
2. Place the cod or haddock fillets skin-side down on a piece of lightly greased foil on a baking tray and bake for 5 minutes.
3. Mix the oil, parsley and garlic in a bowl. Remove tray from the oven and spread the parsley mixture over the surface of the fish.
4. Sprinkle with pine nuts and return to the oven for a further 5 minutes, or until the fish is cooked and the pine nuts are lightly browned. Serve with steamed broccoli.

Broccoli is fantastic for weight loss. Simply steam for 2–3 minutes.

Steamed sea bass with lemon and asparagus

Small bamboo steamers are very inexpensive and make cooking fish so simple. Fish is not only good for you, but it is also very quick to cook. If you can't get sea bass, try red mullet or another firm white fish.

SERVES 2 | PREP TIME 5 MINUTES
COOKING TIME 8 MINUTES
1 bunch asparagus, trimmed
4 sea bass fillets (approx. 120g each)
1 lemon, sliced
1 stalk lemon grass
125g baby spinach leaves
10 cherry tomatoes
1 handful fresh basil
1 tbsp basil oil

1. Arrange the asparagus in a bamboo steamer basket over a pan of boiling water. Place the fish on top, then the lemon slices and lemon grass.
2. Steam for 6–8 minutes, or until the asparagus is just cooked and the fish appears a milky-white colour.
3. Place the spinach, cherry tomatoes and basil on 2 serving plates, and lift the asparagus and fish on top of the salad.
4. Drizzle the basil oil over and serve.

Mediterranean fish stew

SERVES 2 | PREP TIME 5 MINUTES
COOKING TIME 25 MINUTES
1 tbsp olive oil
1 tbsp water
1 medium onion, chopped
1 fennel bulb, cored and shredded
2 garlic cloves, crushed
400g can chopped tomatoes
1 tbsp tomato puree
450ml boiling water
1 tsp organic vegetable bouillon powder
pinch of saffron threads (optional)
half a teaspoon dried mixed herbs
1 fresh cod fillet (150g), skinned and cut into large cubes
1 fresh salmon fillet (150g), skinned and cut into large cubes
zest of orange, grated
4 tbsp chopped fresh parsley
1 small garlic clove, peeled and chopped

1. Heat the oil and water in a large saucepan and cook the onion
gently for 3–4 minutes, or until it begins to soften. Add the fennel
and cook for a further 3 minutes. Then add the garlic and cook
for a few seconds before adding the tomatoes and tomato puree.
2. Add the bouillon, saffron, if desired, and herbs. Stir well and
bring to the boil, then cover with a lid, reduce the heat and
simmer for 15 minutes.
3. Then add the fish, cover the pan again and cook for
6–7 minutes.
4. Mix together the orange, parsley and garlic and set to one side.
Once the stew is ready, garnish with the orange mixture and
serve with a big green salad.

If you would like to add saffron, but haven't any, then substitute
a pinch of turmeric.

LIGHT MEALS

Baked vegetables and quinoa

SERVES 2 | PREP TIME 10 MINUTES
COOKING TIME 30 MINUTES
1 yellow pepper, cut into chunky pieces
1 orange pepper, cut into chunky pieces
1 courgette, sliced
1 red onion, cut into wedges
1–2 tbsp olive oil
2 tbsp pine nuts
60g quinoa grains, rinsed and drained
75g mixed salad leaves
1 lemon, cut into wedges

1. Preheat oven to 250C/gas mark 6.
2. Toss the pepper, courgette and red onion on a baking tray.
3. Drizzle with oil and bake for 25 minutes, adding the pine nuts 5 minutes before it is ready.
4. While these are baking, cook the rinsed and drained quinoa grains in boiling water for 10 minutes, or until tender. Drain well, toss with the salad leaves and transfer to plates.
5. Remove the veggies from the oven and add to the quinoa and salad. Serve with wedges of lemon for squeezing over it.

Brown rice seaweed salad

SERVES 2 | PREP TIME 5 MINUTES
COOKING TIME 20 MINUTES
150g brown rice
1 onion, chopped
1 tsp vegetable oil
1 tbsp water
2cm piece fresh ginger, grated
1 tsp turmeric
2 tbsp chopped fresh parsley
50g seaweed

1. Rinse the rice in cold water then place in a pan of water, bring to the boil, cover and simmer for 15–20 minutes.
2. Place the onion, oil and water in a non-stick frying pan and cook over a moderate heat for 3–4 minutes. Add the ginger and turmeric and cook for a further 2–3 minutes. Remove from the heat and allow to cool.
3. Drain the rice and stir in the onion mixture, parsley and seaweed.
4. Serve either warm or cold.

Chicory stuffed with avocado and tofu

SERVES 2 | PREP TIME 5 MINUTES
1 ripe avocado
125g silken tofu
2 garlic cloves, peeled
4 tbsp lemon juice
2 tbsp chopped fresh parsley
8 chicory or endive leaves
1 handful sprouting fresh mung beans

1. Place the avocado, tofu, garlic, lemon juice and parsley in a food processor and blend until smooth.
2. Spoon the mixture into the chicory or endive leaves and garnish with the sprouting mung beans. Serve immediately.

Cannellini bean salad with baby spinach and oriental herbs

This is quick to make, but packed with flavour. Take the dressing to work in a screw-top jar and the salad in a tupperware box and you have an instant lunch. Another option is to serve with a mug of instant miso soup.

SERVES 2 | PREP TIME 5 MINUTES
400g cannellini beans (drained weight)
100g baby spinach
1 small red onion, finely diced
1 garlic clove, peeled and crushed
1 tbsp chopped fresh coriander
1 tbsp chopped fresh mint
1 tbsp lemon grass, thinly sliced
half-cm piece fresh ginger, grated
a few drops of sesame oil
1 tbsp tamari sauce
1 tbsp lime juice

1. Place the beans, spinach and onion in a salad bowl.
2. Put all the remaining ingredients in a screw-top jar and shake well.
3. Just before serving, pour the dressing over the vegetables and toss well. Serve immediately.

Baked aubergine with quinoa and pine nuts

SERVES 2 | PREP TIME 10 MINUTES
COOKING TIME 30 MINUTES
120g quinoa
350ml cold water
half a teaspoon garam masala/mixed spice
1 large aubergine (400g)
1 tsp olive oil
2 tbsp pine nuts
100g cherry tomatoes, halved
2 tbsp chopped fresh parsley
1 tbsp chopped fresh mint
2 garlic cloves, baked (see below)
juice of half a lemon

1. Place the quinoa, water and spice in a small pan. Bring to the boil, cover and simmer for 20 minutes, or until tender.
2. Preheat the oven to 200C/gas mark 6.
Slice the aubergine in half and score it with a criss-cross pattern using a sharp knife. Carefully oil the cut surface with a pastry brush.
3. Place the aubergine with the cut sides up on a baking tray. Cook in the oven for 10 minutes, and after 6 minutes add the pine nuts to the tray. Keep an eye on them though as you want them golden in colour rather than brown. Remove from the oven and allow the aubergine and pine nuts to cool.
4. Strain the quinoa, place in a bowl and then add all the other ingredients, except the aubergine.
5. Scoop out the flesh of the aubergines using a spoon, chop finely and add to the other ingredients. Mix well. Scoop the filling back into the aubergine shells and serve at room temperature or cold.

Baked garlic

Baking whole bulbs of garlic makes the cloves sweet and soft, and takes away the harshness. Simply place a whole bulb on a baking tray and put in a preheated oven (200C/gas mark 6) for 15 minutes. Remove the cloves from the bulb and the flesh can simply be squeezed out.

Stuffed courgettes

**SERVES 2 | PREP TIME 5–7 MINUTES
COOKING TIME 10 MINUTES**
2 medium-sized courgettes
250g brown rice (cooked)
6 tomatoes, deseeded and chopped
2 tbsp chopped fresh basil
2 garlic cloves, crushed
2 tbsp pine nuts
1 tsp cumin
200ml tomato juice
1 yellow pepper, finely diced

1. Preheat the oven to 180C/gas mark 4.

2. Halve the courgettes and remove the seeds with a teaspoon.

3. Mix together the rice, tomatoes, basil, garlic, pine nuts and cumin and spoon into the centre of the courgettes. Place in a non-stick casserole dish, which has a lid, and pour the tomato juice over them.

4. Bake for 10 minutes in the oven. Transfer to 2 serving plates, scatter the pepper over as garnish and serve immediately.

Moroccan-style chickpea salad

SERVES 2 (AS A LIGHT MEAL) OR 4 (AS A SIDE DISH)
PREP TIME 10 MINUTES | COOKING TIME 30 MINUTES

100g brown rice
2 tbsp olive oil
2 tbsp water
1 medium onion, sliced
1 leek, sliced
1 garlic clove, peeled and crushed
1 tsp ground cumin
half a teaspoon ground coriander
half a teaspoon cinnamon powder
400g can chickpeas, drained and rinsed in cold water
50g fresh peas
juice of 1 lemon
2 tbsp chopped fresh coriander
50g baby spinach leaves

1. Place the rice in a medium-sized pan of water, bring to the boil, cover and simmer for 20–25 minutes, or until tender.
2. Meanwhile, heat the oil and water in a medium-sized frying pan, add the onion and leek, and cook gently for 3 minutes. Stir in the garlic and spices, then cook for a further 2 minutes, stirring regularly. Remove from the heat and allow to cool.
3. Drain the cooked rice and rinse in cold water.
4. Transfer the rice to a large bowl and add the spiced onion mixture, chickpeas, peas, lemon juice and coriander.
5. Arrange the spinach leaves on a serving plate and top with the salad.

This salad can be made in advance and it will keep well in the fridge, covered, for 2–3 days.

Avocado green salad

SERVES 2 | **PREP TIME 2–3 MINUTES**
COOKING TIME 4–5 MINUTES
100g asparagus tips
250g jar organic artichoke hearts in cold pressed oil
1 avocado, peeled, stoned and sliced
juice of 1 lemon
100g mixed salad leaves, such as rocket, watercress or mizuno
1 tbsp chopped fresh chervil

1. Steam the asparagus tips for 4–5 minutes, dependent on the thickness of the tips, then rinse in cold water to preserve the vitamins and colour.
2. While the asparagus is steaming, drain the artichokes, but save the oil and keep to one side.
3. Arrange the avocado on 2 plates in a fan shape.
4. Mix the lemon juice and 2 tablespoons of the reserved oil in a small bowl or screw-top jar.
5. Add the artichoke, asparagus and mixed leaves to the plates, then drizzle over the dressing, garnish with chervil and serve.

Beef tomatoes stuffed with quinoa

This is a very versatile dish that can be served warm or kept in the fridge until the next day. If you're not on my weight-loss plan then you could add a little goat's cheese to step 4.

SERVES 2 | PREP TIME 5 MINUTES
COOKING TIME 25 MINUTES
200g quinoa
400ml boiling water
1 tsp vegetable bouillon powder
1 small onion, chopped
1 garlic clove, peeled and crushed
2 tsp olive oil
1 tbsp water
1 red pepper, diced
1 courgette, diced
2 large beef tomatoes
60g corn kernels
1 handful fresh basil leaves

1. Place the quinoa in a saucepan, add the boiling water and vegetable stock and stir well. Bring to the boil, cover and simmer for 20 minutes.
2. Place the onion and garlic in a non-stick pan together with the oil and water. Cook over a moderate heat until soft and translucent, then add the pepper and courgette, cover and simmer for 3–4 minutes, or until soft.
3. Meanwhile, cut the top off the tomatoes, scoop out the seeds using a spoon and discard. Leave to one side.
4. Remove the vegetables from the heat. Add the corn kernels, basil and quinoa mixture and stir well.
5. Spoon this into the tomatoes and serve while still warm. Alternatively, allow it to cool, keep in the fridge and serve cold.

Hearty miso soup with buckwheat noodles

SERVES 2 | PREP TIME 8–10 MINUTES
COOKING TIME 3–4 MINUTES
25g buckwheat or fine brown rice noodles
500ml boiling water
50g mangetout, trimmed and halved
50g baby corn, trimmed and sliced diagonally
50g fresh or frozen peas
2 sachets instant miso soup
2 spring onions, trimmed and sliced
1 green bok choy, washed and shredded
2 handfuls bean sprouts, rinsed
a few sprigs fresh coriander (optional)

1. Soak the noodles in warm water for 3 minutes, or according to the instructions on the packet. Drain and leave to one side.

2. Add the water, mangetout, baby corn and peas to a medium saucepan, bring it to the boil and cook for just 1 minute.

3. Stir in the instant miso soup, spring onions, bok choy and noodles.

4. Heat through gently for 1–2 minutes, then ladle into deep bowls. Top with bean sprouts and fresh coriander, if desired, and serve.

Mung dhal

This version of the classic Indian dish is real comfort food.
The texture needs to be a little soupy, but not at all watery,
so add liquid as required and do not allow it to dry out.

**SERVES 2 | PREP TIME 5–10 MINUTES
COOKING TIME 45 MINUTES**

250g mung dhal
350ml water
1 small onion, finely chopped
20g tomatoes, cut into quarters and deseeded
3 garlic cloves, chopped
5 cardamom pods
half a teaspoon ginger powder
half of a teaspoon cumin
half of a teaspoon turmeric
1 tsp vegetable oil
2 tbsp water
2 spring onions, chopped

1. Place the mung dhal and water in a medium-sized pan, bring
to the boil and skim any white scum off the surface. Allow to
simmer gently while preparing the onion and tomato mixture.
2. Place the onion, tomatoes, garlic, seasonings, oil and water in
a non-stick pan. Cook over a moderate heat, stirring frequently,
until the onion, tomato and garlic have softened.
3. Add this mixture to the mung dhal. Continue to simmer over
a low heat, stirring occasionally and adding more water as
required, for 30–40 minutes, or until the lentils have split open.
4. Scatter the spring onions over as garnish and serve.

Red warmer lentil salad

SERVES 2 | PREP TIME 3 MINUTES
COOKING TIME 15 MINUTES
100g red lentils
2 shallots
2 garlic cloves
1 tsp chopped fresh ginger
2 tsp wheat-free vegetable bouillon powder
100g fresh rocket
2 tbsp chopped fresh coriander
4 lime wedges

1. Rinse and drain the lentils. Place them in a medium-sized saucepan. Add the shallots, ginger and bouillon powder and cover in cold water. Bring to the boil, then lower and simmer for 12 minutes, stirring occasionally.
2. Remove from the heat and drain away any excess water.
3. Divide the rocket leaves between 2 serving plates and pile the red lentils on top.
4. Garnish with coriander and serve with lime wedges, for squeezing over.

You will probably have enough left over for a side dish or snack. It will keep well in the fridge for up to 3 days.

Braised tofu with shiitake mushrooms

This delicious casserole is ideal for those of you who don't believe you are a fan of tofu. The flavour and texture of the mushrooms, combined with the other ingredients, makes this a fantastic-tasting dish.

SERVES 2 | PREP TIME 5 MINUTES
COOKING TIME 20 MINUTES
200g firm tofu
100g fresh shiitake mushrooms
400ml boiling water
1 tsp miso paste
2 tsp soy sauce
4 spring onions, chopped
2 garlic cloves, chopped
3cm piece fresh ginger, peeled and chopped
3 tbsp flat leaf parsley
40g fresh rocket

1. Preheat the oven to 180C/gas mark 4.
2. Place the tofu and mushrooms in a casserole dish.
3. Mix the miso paste with boiling water, and add the soy sauce, spring onions, garlic, ginger and parsley.
4. Pour over the tofu and mushrooms. Cover it, transfer to the oven and bake for 20 minutes. Scatter with the rocket leaves and serve.

Salad of hearts of palm with pine nuts

This salad has a great crunchy texture and makes a quick and easy lunch – delicious with a cup of vegetable soup. If you make it the day before then keep the nuts separate and sprinkle over just before serving.

SERVES 2 | PREP TIME 3 MINUTES
COOKING TIME 2 MINUTES
2 tbsp pine nuts
220g tinned hearts of palm (drained weight)
quarter of a cucumber, finely diced
1 tbsp chopped fresh parsley
2 tbsp cider vinegar
1 tbsp olive oil

1. Cook the pine nuts over a moderate heat for a few minutes in a non-stick pan (without oil), until they are nicely golden in colour – keep an eye on them, as they will burn very quickly. Remove from the heat and allow to cool.
2. Cut the hearts of palm into bite-size pieces. Place in a bowl and add the cucumber and parsley.
3. Pour the oil and vinegar in a screw-top jar and shake well. Pour over the salad.
4. Just before serving add the pine nuts.

Poached chicken with avocado

Galangel is a root similar to ginger, which aids digestion and is a healthy alternative. It's available in most health food shops and large supermarkets, but if you can't find it then ginger is a suitable substitute.

SERVES 2 | PREP TIME 5 MINUTES
COOKING TIME 30 MINUTES
500ml boiling water
1 vegetable stock cube
1 leek, white part only, cut into fine julienne or sticks
1 medium carrot, peeled and cut into fine julienne or sticks
1 celery stalk, finely sliced
1 bay leaf
2cm piece of galangel or 1 tsp galangel paste(or 2cm piece fresh ginger, finely sliced, or 1 tsp ginger paste)
2–3 kaffir lime leaves
1 lemon grass stalk
1 garlic clove, peeled and sliced
2 tbsp fresh coriander, plus more to garnish
2 skinless chicken breasts (100–125g each)
2 baby bok choy
1 avocado, peeled, stoned and sliced
juice of 1 orange
125g mixed leaves

1. Place the water and stock in a medium-sized pan with a tight-fitting lid and bring to the boil. Add the leek, carrot, celery, bay leaf, ginger, galangel, kaffir lime leaves, lemon grass, garlic and coriander. Simmer for at least 5 minutes to allow the flavours to infuse.

2. Add the chicken and continue to simmer for 8–10 minutes, until the chicken feels firm to the touch.

3. Remove the breasts from the stock, place on a warm plate and leave for 5–10 minutes to rest.

4. Bring the stock back to the boil and reduce the volume to about half.

5. Slice the breasts into 3 pieces and return to the warm plate with the bok choy and avocado.

6. Add the orange juice to the stock.

Spoon some stock and vegetables over the chicken and sprinkle with fresh coriander. Serve immediately with the mixed leaves.

Thai chicken salad

Salad is a very loose translation from the Thai, as many
Thai 'salads' consist of cooked meat, which is served cold on
a bed of cabbage and raw vegetables, with a tasty dressing.
This is a very simple dish, easy to prepare and full of flavour.
If possible, marinate the chicken for 24 hours before cooking.

**SERVES 2 | PREP TIME 5 MINUTES
(PLUS 1-24 HOURS TO MARINATE)
COOKING TIME 10 MINUTES**
300g chicken fillets
2 tbsp tamari sauce
1 tbsp brown rice miso
1 garlic clove, peeled and sliced
1 tsp ginger paste
1 tsp galangel paste
75ml boiling water
1 sachet miso soup
4 kaffir lime leaves
quarter of a Chinese cabbage
1 carrot, cut into matchsticks or julienne
1 red pepper, thinly sliced
2 spring onions, chopped
1 handful bean sprouts
1 handful fresh coriander
1 handful sesame seeds

1. Dissolve the miso soup sachet in boiling water and then
allow to cool.
2. Mix together the tamari sauce, brown rice miso, garlic, ginger,
galangel and miso soup and water. Pour over the chicken fillets
to marinate for at least 1 hour, but preferably leave overnight.
3. Heat a non-stick pan. Remove the chicken from the marinade,
place in the pan and cook for 3–4 minutes, or until the chicken is
firm and white.
4. Remove chicken from the pan and replace with the marinade.
Cook for a few minutes to reduce the volume to about half.
5. Toss all the remaining ingredients together and then add
the hot marinade.
6. Divide between 2 plates and pile the chicken on top. Scatter
over the sesame seeds to garnish and serve.

Sashimi salad with lime ginger vinaigrette

SERVES 2 | PREP TIME 10 MINUTES (PLUS HALF AN HOUR TO MARINATE)

1 piece salmon (approx. 200g)
zest and juice of 2 limes
1 tsp fresh ginger, grated
100g bean sprouts
quarter of a cucumber, finely sliced
5cm piece daikon or mouli, peeled and grated
half a teaspoon wasabi
1 tbsp tamari sauce
2 tsp olive oil
4 lime wedges
2 tsp pickled ginger to garnish

1. Cut the salmon into very fine slices using a sharp knife. Mix the juice and zest of the limes with the ginger, pour it over the salmon and leave to marinate for at least half an hour.
2. Mix the bean sprouts, cucumber and daikon together. Drain the lime juice from the salmon and pour into a small bowl with the wasabi, tamari sauce and olive oil. Mix it all together, pour over the salad and toss well.
3. Arrange the salmon on 2 plates and pile the salad next to the fish. Garnish with lime wedges and pickled ginger and serve.

Very easy tuna salad

SERVES 2 | PREP TIME 5 MINUTES
1 small bag watercress, rocket and spinach salad
200g can tuna steak in spring water, drained
75g cucumber, sliced
8 cherry tomatoes, halved
1 handful mixed olives in olive oil, drained (optional)
2 tbsp extra virgin olive oil
1 tsp good quality balsamic vinegar

Shake the salad leaves over 2 plates and divide the tuna between
them. Add the cucumber and tomatoes, and the olives if desired.
Drizzle oil and vinegar over the salads, and serve.

Pacific-style tuna

Invest in a really good non-stick pan and you will not need any oil to cook fish, meat or vegetables. This dish is served with wasabi, ginger and tamari sauce. Add as much or as little wasabi and ginger as desired to the tamari and use as a dipping sauce for the fish.

SERVES 2 | PREP TIME 5 MINUTES
COOKING TIME 10 MINUTES
2 tuna steaks (125g each)
1 tbsp sesame seeds
150g watercress
50g rocket
4 spring onions, chopped
50g bean sprouts
half a cucumber
2 tbsp brown rice vinegar
a few drops of sesame oil
1 tsp wasabi
1 tsp pickled ginger
2 tbsp tamari sauce
cherry tomatoes
1 handful fresh coriander
lime wedges

1. Coat the tuna well with a generous portion of sesame seeds.
2. Heat a non-stick pan with no oil and, once hot, add the fish. Cook each side for 4–5 minutes.
3. While the fish is cooking toss the watercress, rocket, spring onions and cucumber together with the brown rice vinegar and sesame oil.
4. Arrange the wasabi, ginger and tamari sauce in a small dish.
5. Pile the salad on 2 plates and arrange the tuna to one side, garnished with the tomatoes, coriander and lime wedges.

SIDE DISHES

Asparagus and shiitake mushrooms with mixed vegetables

The colours in this dish are stunning and it tastes great too. Use fresh shiitake mushrooms, which are available in large supermarkets and good greengrocers

SERVES 2 | PREP TIME 3 MINUTES
COOKING TIME 5–7 MINUTES
100g asparagus tips
50g baby corn
1 red pepper, thinly sliced
50g shiitake mushrooms, sliced
60g cucumber, halved, deseeded and sliced
6 spring onions, sliced
50g bean sprouts
2 tbsp chopped fresh coriander
2 tbsp lime juice
2 tsp sesame or olive oil
1 tsp fish sauce
1 garlic clove, peeled and crushed

1. Steam the asparagus and baby corn for 5–7 minutes, depending on the thickness of the asparagus spears.
2. While the asparagus and corn are steaming, prepare the other vegetables and place in a large salad bowl with the coriander.
3. Pour the lime juice, oil, fish sauce and garlic in a screw-top jar and shake well.
4. Add the asparagus and corn to the salad bowl and pour over the dressing. Toss well and serve immediately.

Chickpeas with cauliflower, lemon and capers

SERVES 2 | PREP TIME 5 MINUTES
COOKING TIME 5–7 MINUTES
200g cauliflower florets
200g organic tinned chickpeas (drained weight)
1 tbsp capers
juice of half a lemon
2 tbsp olive oil

1. Steam the cauliflower florets for 5–7 minutes, or until tender
when pierced with a knife.
2. Place the cauliflower in a bowl whilst still warm and add all the
other ingredients. Toss well and serve at room temperature.

This salad improves if left to stand for at least half an hour before
eating. It can also be made the day before and kept in the fridge.
Allow the salad to return to room temperature before eating.

White cabbage slaw with cashew and caraway

SERVES 2 | PREP TIME 5 MINUTES
1 small white cabbage (approx. 450g), cored and finely sliced
1 small onion (approx. 50g), chopped
1 medium carrot (approx. 50g), grated
caper, coriander and tofu dressing (see p. 202)
2 tsp caraway seeds
2 tbsp cashew nuts, roughly chopped

1. Put the cashew nuts to one side and mix all the other ingredients
together in a plastic bowl with a fitted lid.
2. Keep in the fridge until required, and scatter with the reserved
nuts just before serving. It keeps well for up to 5 days

Beetroot with hemp

SERVES 2 | PREP TIME 3–4 MINUTES
COOKING TIME 20–30 MINUTES
200g beetroot
2 tbsp hemp oil
2 tbsp cider vinegar
2 tbsp raw shelled hemp seeds
sprig of dill

1. Trim the leaves of the beetroot about 5 cm from the root. Place the beetroot in a pan of cold water, bring to the boil and simmer for 20–30 minutes, or until tender when pierced with a knife.
2. Pour the oil and vinegar in a screw-top jar and shake well.
3. Peel the beetroot, dice into 1–2-cm cubes and place in a serving bowl.
4. Drizzle over the dressing, scatter with the seeds and garnish with dill. Serve immediately.

Courgette Salad with Lemon and Dill

SERVES 2 | PREP TIME 5 MINUTES (PLUS CHILLING TIME)
4 courgettes, finely sliced
zest and juice of 1 lemon
2 garlic cloves, crushed
3 tbsp chopped fresh dill
2 tsp olive oil

1. Place all the ingredients in a plastic container with a tight-fitting lid. Shake well and leave in the fridge for at least 12 hours.
2. Serve with a portion of brown rice or quinoa.

Slice the courgette as thinly as possible – if you have a mandolin that would be ideal. This salad improves in flavour if made in advance and it keeps well in the fridge for 3 days.

Fennel salad with cucumber, red onion and celery

This is a great crunchy fresh salad, ideal as a lunch or an accompaniment to a dinner dish.

SERVES 2 | PREP TIME 10 MINUTES
COOKING TIME 20 MINUTES
100g quinoa
200ml boiling water
half a teaspoon vegetable bouillon powder
200g fennel, halved, cored and finely sliced
50g red onion, halved and finely sliced
100g celery, finely sliced
100g cucumber, halved, deseeded and finely sliced
2 tbsp olive oil
2 tbsp cider vinegar
juice of half a lemon

1. Place the quinoa, water and stock in a small saucepan. Bring to the boil, then cover and simmer for 20 minutes.
2. Place the fennel, red onion, celery and cucumber in a bowl.
3. Drain the quinoa and add to the fennel salad.
4. Pour the oil, vinegar and lemon juice into a screw-top jar, shake well, drizzle over the salad and serve.

Tomato salad with puy lentils and herb dressing

SERVES 2 | PREP TIME 5 MINUTES
6 vine-ripened tomatoes
320g tinned puy lentils (drained weight)
1 small red onion, finely chopped
1 tsp Dijon mustard
1 tbsp cider vinegar
3 tbsp olive oil
2 tbsp chopped fresh basil, plus extra leaves
1 tbsp chopped fresh parsley

1. Arrange the tomatoes on a serving plate.

2. Drain the lentils and mix with the onion, mustard, vinegar, oil and herbs.

3. Pile on to the tomatoes and garnish with the basil leaves.

Purple sprouting broccoli with sesame

SERVES 2 | PREP TIME 3–4 MINUTES
COOKING TIME 4–5 MINUTES
1 tsp sesame oil
1 tbsp water
200g purple sprouting broccoli, trimmed
2 tsp tamari sauce
1 tbsp sesame seeds

1. Place the oil and water in a wok or frying pan, heat for 1 minute and then add the broccoli.
2. Cook for 3–4 minutes, tossing or stirring regularly, and then add the sesame seeds. Cook for a further 30 seconds, add the tamari sauce and serve immediately.

DIPS

Aduki beans with red onion and corn salsa

Aduki beans are now available in cans from all health food shops and large supermarkets. For a change, you can always substitute black-eyed peas. This dish makes a great salsa to serve with oily fish such as salmon or mackerel. It also makes a great snack or quick lunch. As an option, add a little hemp oil to taste.

SERVES 2 | PREP TIME 2–3 MINUTES
175g tinned aduki beans (drained weight)
80g can organic sweet corn
75g red onion, finely chopped
2 tbsp cider vinegar

Mix all the ingredients together and serve.

Black-eyed pea hummus

Tahini is an oily paste that is extracted from sesame seeds and it gives a lovely kick to this hummus. It is available in health food shops and large supermarkets.

SERVES 2 | PREP TIME 5 MINUTES
350g can black-eyed peas
2 tbsp tahini
2 garlic cloves, peeled
juice of 1 lemon
1 tbsp fresh parsley leaves

1. Place all the ingredients in a food processor and blend until you have a fairly smooth paste. Transfer to a small bowl and keep covered in the fridge until required.
2. This makes a great dip with raw vegetable sticks and it keeps well in the fridge for 3 days.

Cashew and Brazil nut paté

SERVES 4–6 | PREP TIME 5 MINUTES
100g plain Brazil nuts, roughly chopped
100g plain cashew nuts, roughly chopped
2 tsp olive oil
1 garlic clove, peeled and roughly chopped
1 tbsp freshly squeezed lemon juice
1 handful fresh parsley (approx. 5g)
4 tbsp water

Whiz all the ingredients together in a food processor until almost smooth. You may need to remove the lid and push the mixture down a few times to get the right consistency. Serve with lots of fresh vegetable sticks. This will keep well in the fridge for up to 2 days.

Mashed avocado with hummus

SERVES 2 | PREP TIME 5 MINUTES
1 large or 2 small ripe avocados, stoned and peeled
410g tinned chickpeas (drained weight)
2 garlic cloves
juice of 1 lemon

Place all the ingredients in a food processor and blend until smooth. Cover well and keep in the fridge for 1 day.

DRESSINGS

Caper, coriander and tofu dressing

MAKES 100ML | PREP TIME 5 MINUTES
50ml olive oil
45g silken tofu
6g small capers
1 tbsp chopped fresh coriander
40ml lemon juice
half a garlic clove, peeled and crushed

Place all the ingredients in a blender or food processor and blend until smooth. Transfer to a screw-top jar and refrigerate until required. It will keep for 5 days.

Chervil and spring onion dressing

MAKES 85ML | PREP TIME 5 MINUTES
50ml olive oil
1 tbsp cider vinegar
1 spring onion, chopped
1 tbsp chopped chervil

Place all the ingredients in a screw-top jar and shake well. It is best made 2–3 hours before required to allow the flavours to infuse. Keep refrigerated for 3 days.

Tasty tomato and pepper sauce

This quick sauce is a great all-rounder and goes brilliantly with burgers, grilled meat and fish.

MAKES 450ML | PREP TIME 5 MINUTES
COOKING TIME 16–20 MINUTES
1 tbsp olive oil
1 tbsp water
1 medium onion, finely chopped
2 garlic cloves, peeled and crushed
1 orange pepper, deseeded and cut into 1-cm pieces
400g can chopped tomatoes
half a teaspoon dried mixed herbs

1. Heat the oil and water in a medium-sized saucepan and sauté the onion and garlic gently for 3 minutes, stirring regularly, until softened but not coloured. Add the pepper and cook for a further 2 minutes.

2. Stir in the tomatoes, then fill half the empty can with cold water and tip into the pan. Add the herbs and bring to the boil, then reduce the heat and simmer gently for 10–15 minutes, stirring occasionally, until the vegetables are tender and the sauce is thick.

If reserving half the sauce to use in another recipe, allow to cool, then cover and chill until required. It will last in the fridge for up to 2 days.

Cheese-free pesto dressing

MAKES 225ML | PREP TIME 5 MINUTES
100ml extra virgin olive oil
1 large handful fresh basil leaves (approx. 60g)
50g pine nuts
1 plump garlic clove, peeled
2 tsp lemon juice, freshly squeezed
2 tbsp water

1. Place all the ingredients in a food processor and blend until smooth – you may need to push the mixture down a couple of times. Allow 1–2 tablespoons of pesto per person.

It can be used as a gutsy salad dressing, tossed through warmed mixed beans or served as a dip with fresh, crunchy vegetables. I adore this full-flavoured dressing and always keep some basil handy in case I want to make it. You'll need roughly 1 large basil plant to get the 60 g. Add a little more water if you like a thinner dressing, as this one also doubles up as a dip. If tightly covered, it will keep in the fridge for 1–2 days.

Chive and lime dressing

This is a clean, fresh-tasting dressing and is ideal for raw summer vegetables such as fennel or chicory.

MAKES 80ML | PREP TIME 5 MINUTES
50ml extra virgin olive oil
1 tbsp chopped fresh chives
15ml lime juice
10ml cider vinegar

Place all the ingredients together in a screw-top jar and shake well. Keep refrigerated for up to 3 days.

SNACKS

Snacking is good for you. Do it three times a day: mid morning, mid afternoon and evening too. There are endless ideas when it comes to snacks. Here are a few ideas. Do get creative when it comes to your snacks.

- ❤ Any fruit
- ❤ Any vegetable
- ❤ Chicory lined with hummous and baby tomatoes
- ❤ Gem lettuce lined with dip and chopped pepppers
- ❤ Vegetable sticks and crudités with dips, pâtés and spreads
- ❤ Dates
- ❤ Raw shelled hemp seeds
- ❤ Sunflower seeds
- ❤ Nuts and soaked nuts too. When you soak your nuts overnight, they are so easy to digest
- ❤ Steamed nuts
- ❤ Sauerkraut
- ❤ Sprouted seeds and sprouted grains
- ❤ Soaked chickpeas
- ❤ Toasted nori strips
- ❤ Baked sweet potatoes with mashed avocado
- ❤ Mashed avocado
- ❤ Freshly squeezed fruit juice
- ❤ Vegetable juice
- ❤ Smoothies
- ❤ Sprouted hemp bread
- ❤ Pumpkin seeds

PART 3 ONE WEEK TO GO

LOOK HOW FAR YOU'VE COME!

Doesn't time fly? It's one week to go until you say, 'I do.' Excited? You should be – I'm excited *for* you!

Now don't worry, because I've still got plenty of advice to give you to help you through this final week. I'll be telling you what to eat and drink to help you get a good night's sleep, to minimize nerves, and how to approach the day itself feeling light and energetic and full of joy.

But before we move on to that, let's take some time to look at how far you've come and what you've achieved. Once you realize the impact my Wedding Countdown has made on how you look and feel, the spirit of confidence and celebration will just come pouring out of you, making you an even more beautiful bride.

In Part One I promised that you if you stuck to my plan you would:

1 Lose weight
2 Reduce cellulite and eliminate bloating
3 Digest food easily
4 Have heaps more energy
5 Cope easily with wedding-planning stress
6 Suffer less from PMS and low moods
7 Be less susceptible to colds and flu, thanks to a bolstered immune system
8 Have a glowing complexion, glossy hair and strong nails
9 Feel more sexy
10 Boost your fertility

See? I told you. I stick to my promises.

I also asked you to record your measurements and how you feel. Let's try that exercise again now, but, please, make this the very last time that you weigh yourself.

I do not believe in scales or weighing. It's all tied in with calorie counting and food number crunching. Weighing and counting is so last century. Weighing and scales lead to an obsession with numbers and very often a negative relationship with food.

What you should be thinking about is how you feel about yourself, your health and energy levels. By now, you will have developed a much more positive image about yourself and I know you will be feeling a lot better. As for the weight, it will definitely be coming off. If you have done everything to the letter, my way, you will be shifting the weight in good style. You will see your weight loss reflected in your dress size anyway, so you don't need to weigh yourself. But I *know* you brides. I have a funny feeling you can't resist one last jump on the scales. But keep in mind that muscle weighs more than fat, and with all the exercise you will have quite a few more muscles on your bod.

So, I want you to banish for ever (after today) the idea that your weight in numbers has to be a part of your life. Agreed? Excellent.

My Vital Statistics, today:

_ _ / _ _ / _ _ _ _

I weigh: _____

Measurements:

bust _____

waist _____

hips _____

thighs _____

upper arms _____

My skin is: _____

My hair is: _____

My nails are: _____

Other issues: _____

Today, I feel: _____

How do your answers compare with those you wrote down back when you first began this wedding programme? How many pounds and inches have you lost; how much better do you look and feel? (You might like to write down your initial measurements too, in brackets, so you can see the difference.)

And let's think back to those five Wedding Goals you set. If you've been using them as your daily mantras, as I suggested, they should be ingrained on your mind by now. So have you reached your goals? Maybe you've even surpassed them.

For each goal, I want you to write down, below, how much of it you've achieved. Say, for example, your first goal was: 'I am a size 12,' write down below what size you are today. If your second goal was: 'I have heaps more energy,' write down just how energetic you feel right now. Off you go . . .

My Wedding Achievements:

1. _____
2. _____
3. _____
4. _____
5. _____

Finally, flick back to that photograph of yourself, on page 17, before you discovered my way of living. Frightening, isn't it? But that's not you any more. The gorgeous, fit, healthy, glowing, slimmer person you see in the mirror today *is*.

To make sure you never forget, here's another space for you to stick in your 'after' photo. You might want to wait and use one of you on the morning of your wedding, or on the beach on honeymoon. Don't you look just fantastic? Congratulations!

A photo of myself now:

YOUR FINAL WEEK

The last week of your Wedding Countdown might be your busiest week yet, with orders to confirm, flowers to check, beauty appointments to keep, relatives to entertain. Or it might be all quiet on the practical front because you're so organized. And that's when the nerves really start to kick in!

Either way, it's my job to keep you on track. Now the happy-ever-after ending is in sight, it can be tempting to let things slip – to 'forget' your healthy eating and excuse yourself from exercise.

OK, I know it's only seven days and you're not going to pile all the flab back on in such a short time. But reintroducing the nasties may well show on your face, your energy levels and your mood. You've worked so hard, is it worth it?

The key to staying focused is to be prepared. Make sure you have a week's worth of nourishing food at home, so everything you need is to hand. If a well-meaning mother, aunt or chief bridesmaid keeps asking what she can do to help you, send her to the greengrocer's! Or get her to make you lunch or dinner and ask her to prepare some healthy snacks, and then make sure that those are always on hand. Or make exercise

dates with her throughout the week to keep you energized.

I don't want you to panic if you do have social events in your diary for this week – a hen night or rehearsal dinner, say. Enjoy them. Then get right back on track the next morning. Don't waste time feeling guilty or having regrets. (For hen-night damage-limitation tricks, see page 54.)

Finally, a word of warning. Absolutely *no* enemas or colonics the day before or the day of your wedding, please. You are as cleaned out as you need to be at this point. To try to get married on the same day as a major clean-out with a colonic or even an enema is asking too much of your body. If you add in your anxiety and nerves, you could end up tired or cramping in your tummy. And there's no need for that.

Pillow talk

Try to get to bed by 10.30 p.m. every night this week, and get a good eight hours' shut-eye. Studies show that getting to sleep before midnight and having regular sleeping and waking times is healthiest for the body. Sleep is a time of repair and rejuvenation, and a lack of it can cause a hormonal imbalance which can actually lead to cravings and weight gain. You have been warned!

If you're tired, it'll show on your face and in your mood, your feelings of stress and anxiety will be enhanced, your concentration and libido will suffer, your metabolism will slow and you're more likely to cave in and make unhealthy food choices.

To help you drift off to the land of nod:

❤ Eat only light meals or snacks after 6 p.m. Foods rich in magnesium and the amino acid tryptophan are perfect as they help you to relax. So snack on almonds, oatcakes or a green salad – lettuce actually contains chemicals that help you sleep!

❤ Drink valerian, passion flower, linden flower or camomile tea.

❤ Inhale lavender, camomile, clary sage or neroli essential oils. Put a few drops on a tissue and place it under your pillow, or diffuse the oil in an aromatherapy oil burner for an hour or so before bed.

WAKEY WAKEY EYE DEPUFFER

Last-minute jitters kept you up all night? Try this relaxing beauty treat to keep under-eye bags and puffiness at bay.

1 tsp aloe vera gel
1 cm slice of cucumber, peeled
1 tsp witch hazel

Mash the aloe vera and cucumber together with a fork. Mix in the witch hazel. Chill in the fridge in a sealed jar. Using your ring finger, pat a pea-sized amount of gel all around the socket bone of your eyes. Store in the fridge and use within three days.

Handy tip: if you don't have the time or the ingredients to make this gel, slices of cucumber or chilled (wet) camomile tea bags will do wonders too. Close your eyes, lie back and relax for ten minutes with them resting on your eyes.

What to eat on the eve of your wedding

Today is about keeping it simple, filling and easy to digest. Think of delicious foods to nourish your body and mind. Obviously it is best to eat lightly so that digestion does not interfere with your beauty sleep. It is also important to eat *something* as not eating can also lead to poor sleep. I don't want you launching into a one-day detox or starving yourself, or anything silly like that.

Some of you may have a rehearsal dinner tonight. Enjoy yourself, but remember that you need to eat simply. And make sure that you absolutely do not have fruit for dessert if you do go out.

You will only end up bloated and gassy. Do not put too many different foods into your body this evening, and stay away from awkward combinations. Avoid hot spices like chilli, as well as celebratory drinks with lots of bubbles that will only leave you cramping and gassy.

As much as I love you to try new foods, stick with what you know on the eve of your wedding. There's no need to introduce anything new to your regime today.

A meal that will leave you radiant in the morning could include:

Aperitif

Carrot, celery, beetroot and ginger juice – carrots are great for the skin, celery reduces water retention and bloating, beetroot is good for the liver and blood, while ginger aids digestion and reduces nausea (in case you have butterflies in your stomach!). The juice can be a small glass. This is not the time to down a litre of veggie juice.

Starter

Avocado, watercress, rocket and tomato salad with pine nuts – avocados provide the essential fats needed for healthy skin, hair and nails; watercress and rocket contain beta-carotene for eye health and magnesium for relaxation; tomatoes will protect you from bacteria and viruses, while also being the colour of love (tomatoes were once known as 'love apples'). Or have hearty soup – easy to digest and a good filler upper.

Main meal

Salmon with steamed carrots and green beans – salmon provides essential fats for beautiful skin and brain function; the vegetables are a good source of beta-carotene for eye and skin health as well as of magnesium for relaxation and energy. Serve with sprouted seeds. Or for the vegetarians among you: a brown rice seaweed salad (page 168) contains an array of nerve-soothing B vitamins and minerals.

Dessert

Rather than eating a dessert, slather some mashed avocado, oatmeal and honey onto your face for a nourishing face pack. Leave on for twenty minutes and gently wash off for a glowing complexion.

Super Soups

If you are really anxious, just stick to soups, broths and maybe a crunchy salad if you feel up to it, but nothing too heavy. When anxiety ridden, the worst thing you can do is stuff loads of food into your tummy. You won't digest it well and you will end up bloated, gassy and nauseous.

Stress and Gas

When you are stressed out, your digestive system can be a wee bit weaker, so on the day before your wedding avoid potentially gas-forming vegetables such as brussel sprouts, broccoli and cauliflower. If beans and lentils make you gassy, then avoid these today. But for your future reference, if you get gassy from certain foods, then this means that your digestion needs improving.

I must emphasize that these foods will not create gas when you are calm and your digestion is better. My clients never complain of gas from them. So although they are not a problem for everyone, some people lack the enzymes needed to break these foods down really well at first. The day before your wedding is not the time to begin to introduce them into your diet! (Although you should have introduced them ages ago if you were doing what I say; so that's another matter.) If you introduce these foods gradually over a period of time, your body will adapt to them and you will be able to eat them with abandon. Definitely don't eat fruit after your dinner as this can cause fermentation and gas.

Onions and garlic can leave a lingering smell, so don't eat these the day before. If you like hummus, get a garlic-free version for today or pass on that spread.

Don't be tempted by spicy foods as they may irritate the digestive system.

Alcohol and caffeine should also definitely be off your list for now as they will interfere with sleep and leave your skin dehydrated.

Avoid salt and foods containing salt as they could cause water retention and bloating. And needless to say, but I'll say it anyway: wheat, dairy and yeast can cause bloating so these are best avoided.

Your Bridal Breakfast

It's going to be a long day and you may not get to eat anything else until your reception. So DO NOT SKIP BREAKFAST on the morning of your wedding. I know you'll probably wake up with butterflies in your stomach and not feel like feasting. But I insist that you have a sensible, light-but-filling brekkie. Your mother will tell you the same.

The right breakfast will not make your tummy look bloated, make you feel sick or make any of the other worries you may have come true. What it *will* do is:

❤ Line your stomach and prevent you getting tipsy as soon as a sip of champagne touches your lips

❤ Keep you full until your next meal and prevent your stomach gurgling during your vows

❤ Calm your nerves and prevent light-headedness – you don't want to faint as you walk up the aisle

I would suggest you start your day with a cup of warm water, then a cup of nerve-calming, vitamin B-packed nettle tea. Follow this with a mango and banana smoothie. That's 1 mango, 1 banana and 120ml water all blended together until smooth and creamy. Into your serving bowl you can chuck a handful of energy-boosting blueberries or zinc-filled raspberries. Then pour the smoothie over and eat with a spoon. After a good half-hour wait, serve yourself a lovely big bowl of porridge oats or oat bran. Oats are packed with stress-relieving B vitamins and should be enough to tone and relax your nervous system. End result: you will be calm and relaxed.

Remember to really take your time and eat breakfast slowly. My best advice for your bridal breakfast is to eat by yourself and don't talk to anyone during this meal. When people are excited and yacking away at the same time as eating, a lot of air tends to end up in the tummy, creating unnecessary gas. So make this bridal brekkie a solitary experience if you can. Think of it as a little extra 'me' time.

Focus on *Your* Day

So this is it. It's the morning of your long-awaited wedding. You're going to have the time of your life, marry the man of your dreams and be the centre of attention all day and night. And I know from experience that the next twenty-four hours are going to fly by.

So before you rush headlong into this fabulous whirlwind of fun – people fussing around you, taking photographs, wanting to soak up your wonderful aura – start the day with a little meditation exercise to calm your mind, focus your thoughts and just 'be'.

While you can, take half an hour to yourself. Go to the bathroom, put a Do Not Disturb sign outside and lock the door. Run yourself a luxurious bath or take a long, therapeutic shower.

❤ As you lie – or stand – there, close your eyes and take some deep breaths. Imagine a beautiful white rod of light entering your body from above you, through your head.

❤ Inhale and visualize the white light filling your body with positive energy and love.

❤ Exhale and imagine any worries, nerves, tiredness or negativity leaving your body on the out-breath.

❤ Breathe in again and this time, as you breathe out, say the words, 'I am beautiful.'

❤ On the next out-breath, say, 'I am confident.'

❤ And on the next, say, 'I am loved.'

❤ All the while, visualize that white light filling every cell of your body with its positive energy and radiating out into your immediate surroundings.

You can repeat these affirmations as many times as you want.

If at any time during the day you need some calm and stillness, try to find five minutes on your own, breathe deeply and return your mind to the white light.

Now, you're ready to face your public . . .

FAST-ACTING STRESS-RELIEF SUPPLEMENTS

Rescue Remedy – I think this Bach Flower Remedy is a great 'emergency' tonic if you're feeling nervous and tense. Add four drops to a small glass of water and sip at intervals, or put the drops directly onto your tongue. Ask your chief bridesmaid, your father, or someone else who'll be with you right before the ceremony, to keep a bottle of Rescue Remedy handy for you. People might find it useful before their speeches too.

Black Eyed Susan – This is the Australian Bush remedy for stress. It works wonders. Put seven drops under the tongue every morning and night. If you need to, you can take it a couple of times during the day too, in the run-up to your wedding day. Normally you might take this remedy for two to three weeks, stop for a week, then see how you feel and decide whether you still need it.

Rhodiola – This herbal supplement is an adaptogen, like Siberian ginseng, so it helps your body adapt to stress. The wonderful thing about rhodiola, in particular, is that it's so fast-acting. Unlike other herbs, which may take months to show signs of working, this could be taken for the week before your wedding and you would still benefit from its calming effects.

Siberian Ginseng – This is one of the oldest-known herbal remedies, used as an energy tonic for thousands of years.

An adaptogen, it also nourishes tired blood and helps your body adapt to stress. As this is your last week, drink it as a tea (rather than taking supplements) for more immediate effects.

B vitamins – Take a mega B complex daily. This is the anti-stress nutrient. If you've already been taking it for weight-loss purposes, your levels should be fine, so just carry on with your current dose.

Astragalus – This is a vitamin B-packed anti-stress herbal remedy. Even taken only forty-eight hours before the wedding, it would make a difference. Astragalus is known for immune-strengthening properties, so consider it a good preventative for warding off colds and flu. You become more susceptible to viruses and bugs when you are stressed so think of Astragalus as your stress zapper.

Liquid Algae – this is a nutrient-packed superfood in liquid form with practically every nutrient known to man. Liquid algae can help keep your strength up today. I used it when I was in labour. So if it gave me the strength to push out a baby, it can surely help get you down the aisle. Get your mum, bridesmaid or a friend to pop it in her handbag for you. You can take a dropperful when you feel the need for an energy top-up.

For more advice on minimizing stress, see page 104.

HERE COMES THE BRIDE . . .

Well, what can I say? Your fiancé is one lucky man. When he slipped that engagement ring onto your finger, he was already head over heels in love. But when he sees you on your wedding day, you'll take his breath away. Congratulations! You've worked so hard and achieved so much. I'm truly proud of you. You have been well and truly Bridally McKeithed.

When we started out on this journey together, I promised you my programme would be unlike any diet you'd tried (and failed at) before. I promised you that you wouldn't feel hungry or that you were missing out.

I hope you have been opened up to a whole new way of living that brings you happiness and well-being. If you make my wise food choices and take regular exercise, nourishing your body and mind with what they need, you get results. You feel slim, attractive, strong, energetic and, above all, positive.

Now that you've seen these results for yourself, my secret hope is that you'll continue on with me. Although I devised this programme especially for brides, it's a window onto the Gillian McKeith Way of Life. There's more I can share with you. So if you want to continue looking and feeling as fantastic as you do, and would like to deepen your understanding of what it means to be healthy, you know where I am . . .

Many people like to portray me as some sort of militant health tyrant. The thing is, I care that you succeed. I care deeply. But I'm only strict with you because I want you to be the very best you can. I do have a heart, you know!

To prove it, you have my blessing to indulge on your special day. Celebrate your union – and your success – with the finest champagne (not too much, though; and of course there's always non-alcoholic wine, don't forget that!); savour every course of your wedding breakfast; have a big slice of wedding cake. And another if you wish. You've worked hard for it. But I wouldn't be Gillian McKeith if I didn't tell you that wedding cakes can actually be made in healthy versions too. So, if you have the time, see what you can do about that. Then you can eat the whole cake if you want! And, of course, kick off your high heels and dance the night away.

Lisa, one of my recent TV brides, whose wedding I attended, told me that after going on my plan, she knew that she looked and felt ten times better than she had ever expected on her wedding day. She shocked friends and relatives alike because there was such a change. Before she met me, Lisa had cancelled her wedding date twice because she lacked the confidence to walk down the aisle.

She used to joke about having to squeeze sideways between the pews to make it to the altar. When I saw her on her third-time-lucky, very special date, she oozed confidence, was beaming with happiness and bursting with pride instead of bloat. She told me that her pictures and memories are with her for life now and they are really good ones. Not only was her wedding day the best day ever but all the bridal preparation set her on a whole new path for life.

There you have it, girls. It's been a pleasure walking with you on your wedding journey, but now you're at the start of a new journey and it's time for me to let you go. All that remains is for me to wish you a fantastic, wonderful day. I hope you and your husband have a happy, healthy future together, and that you cherish your married life.

Lots of love and light,

Gillian

ACKNOWLEDGEMENTS

Enormous gratitude to all my brides-to-be, who so willingly (and sometimes with a push up the bahookee from me) throw themselves into operation bridal countdown à la Gillian.

A great big special thanks to Hannah for all your hard work. Appreciation to Justine and the gang and a warm hug too. You have a special gift. I think just one more Goji Berry will do it. To everyone at Penguin, including Kate: THANK YOU. It is an amazing journey to change this country's eating habits for the better. Thanks to everyone at Smith & Gilmour for your brilliant design skills. Helen: Lots of Love to you and your family. Who needs scales? We could measure up raw shelled hemp seeds in our sleep. Well done to Zdrafka for cooking up a storm with all my recipes. Luigi. You are a Star. Love to you. And massive appreciation to Nicola, Jo, Julia, Jonny, Helen and Sophie. Love to Murray, Danielle, Charlotte, Jo, Lucy, Jonny, Kelly, Angie and all behind the scenes of our TV brides-to-be. Thanks to Josie too. Continued heartfelt love to Howard for your inspiration and insight.

A big hug and lots of love to all my viewers who tune in every week. Keep watching and spread the word.

Gillian McKeith is a Doctor of Philosophy in Holistic Nutrition (PhD), a qualification gained after several years of study from the American Holistic College of Nutrition, USA (now Clayton College). She is a postgraduate member of the Centre for Nutrition, Education and Lifestyle Management, UK. Before retraining in nutrition, Gillian graduated with a BA from Edinburgh University, UK, and with an MA from the University of Pennsylvania, USA. She has worked for over 15 years in the field of nutrition.

www.drgillianmckeith.com